W.M. Dawson
2/51-

CASS LIBRARY OF VICTORIAN TIMES

No. 6

General Editor: Anne Humpherys

Herbert H. Lehman College, New York

HOMES OF THE LONDON POOR

and

THE BITTER CRY OF OUTCAST LONDON

HOMES

OF

THE LONDON POOR

Octavia Hill

and

THE BITTER CRY OF OUTCAST LONDON

An Inquiry into the Condition of
the Abject Poor

Andrew Mearns

*With a note on the authors
by W. H. Chaloner*

FRANK CASS & CO. LTD,
1970

Published by
FRANK CASS AND COMPANY LIMITED
67 Great Russell Street, London WC1B 3BT

Homes of the London Poor

First published   1875
Second edition   1883
New impression
of Second edition   1970

The Bitter Cry of Outcast London

First published   1883
New impression   1970

ISBN 0 7146 2419 5

Printed in Great Britain by Clarke, Doble & Brendon Ltd.
Plymouth and London

A NOTE ON
'HOMES OF THE LONDON POOR'

Octavia Hill (1838–1912), grand-daughter of the pioneer sanitary reformer, Dr. T. Southwood Smith, came under the influence of the Christian Socialists and John Ruskin in her early teens and by 1864 had developed a profound interest in improving the dwellings of the London poor. Supported by influential and wealthy friends she became a housing manageress in 1865, buying the leases of slum properties and gradually rehabilitating both houses and occupants. Very soon she was appointed by the Ecclesiastical Commissioners to manage the greater part of their properties in Southwark. She became a member of the Charity Organisation Society and took an active part in propaganda for R. A. Cross's Artizans' Dwellings Act of 1875. In that year five magazine articles which she had written were published in pamphlet form under the title *Homes of the London Poor*, and were translated into German by Princess Alice of Hesse. This was Miss Hill's best-known work and the second enlarged edition is now made available again after having been extremely difficult to consult for many years.

A NOTE ON THE AUTHORSHIP OF
'THE BITTER CRY OF OUTCAST LONDON'

Although there has been considerable uncertainty and confusion about the authorship of *The Bitter Cry of Outcast London* (1883), it is now clear that this powerful and influential pamphlet was written by the Rev. William Carnall Preston (1837–1902), a Congregational minister with experience in Wigan at the height of the Lancashire cotton famine, who had also been a newspaper editor for three years (1867–70). The Rev. Andrew Mearns (1837–1925), secretary of the Congregational Union, undertook the field work on which the pamphlet is based, in the summer of 1883, assisted by the Rev. James Munro. The resulting data were then handed over to the Rev. W. C. Preston, presumably because of his expertise as a journalist, and by the autumn he had fully justified the Union's decision by writing a vivid pamphlet on the slums of central London which had an immediate and fruitful impact on public opinion. Evidence of the authorship and influence of *The Bitter Cry* are set forth in P. d'A. Jones, *The Christian Socialist Revival, 1877–1914* (1968), pp. 413–18; S. H. Mayor, *The Churches and the Labour Movement* (1967), p. 56; and K. S. Inglis, *Churches and the Working Classes in Victorian England* (1963).

January, 1970   W.H.C.

HOMES

OF

THE LONDON POOR.

BY

OCTAVIA HILL.

A NEW EDITION.

London:
MACMILLAN AND CO.
1883.

CONTENTS.

V.

VI.

VII.

PREFACE TO FIRST EDITION.

IN reprinting at this time articles describing any scheme for improving the dwellings of the poor, the first thought which suggests itself is, how the question is likely to be affected by the Artisans' Dwellings Bill, which is before the Houses of Parliament, more especially as one of the articles in this book was written in the earnest hope and expectation that some such measure would shortly be brought before the Legislature.

Two principal objections have been made to the Bill. First, the costliness of its procedure. Everyone must desire to see this reduced to the minimum; but where compulsory powers are taken under any Act, many safeguards are, I believe, required, and these imply expensive processes. One can only hope that in this case they will be reduced as far as possible. But there has been a good deal said about the impropriety of supplying a large class of the people with a necessary of life, such as lodging, at a price which is not remunerative.

I enter more deeply, perhaps, than most of the objectors themselves into the full weight of this objection, and most heartily hope that whatever is done in building for the people may be done on a thoroughly sound commercial principle. I do not think it would help them the least in the long run to adopt any other principle; in fact, I believe it would be highly injurious to them.

But let it be distinctly understood that under this Bill two separate processes are contemplated. They come, indeed, under one scheme, and are entrusted in a measure to the same agents; but they are distinctly two. There is the clearing away of old accumulated nuisances which ought never to have been allowed to grow up at all—courts built narrower than Building Acts would now allow; houses with no thorough ventilation, or built on damp soil or without good foundation. Clearing away old abuses cannot pay, except in the sense in which all reform pays. Abolition of slavery didn't pay; the nation had to pay for it. Happy if by mere payment in money it could efface so great a wrong! So it must be with these courts and alleys. It cannot be remunerative in £ s. d. to remove them, neither can you fairly throw the cost on the individual owner; the community—the dulled conscience of which, the ignorance of which, allowed them to grow up—must pay for removing them. But, once cleared, the buildings erected ought to be remunerative; and I earnestly hope no short-sighted benevolence will ever deceive our legislators into losing sight of this.

The second main objection raised to the Bill has been that it is not compulsory enough. As far as that section of the country which calls itself Liberal is concerned, that seems to me a very strange complaint. I have always thought that Conservatives and Liberals worthy of the name, equally bent on achieving the good thing, and having got rid of any hankering to conserve what was evil or care for freedom to do wrong, were divided one from another as to the means, the one believing that government from above marshalled the people on right ways, which they grew to love by following; the other having longer patience, and caring to wait till, by gradual teaching, the people chose voluntarily the right way, and believing that the advances willingly and intelligently made were never lost, and were themselves better training.

At any rate, here we have an "enabling" Bill, as someone well called it. It will put it in our power collectively to clear the foul places away if we wish. Let it be distinctly understood we had not got this power before Mr. Cross's Bill. There are courts beyond courts of the worst kind, in the East-end especially, where there isn't a vestige of a title which would warrant any society or individual in erecting a substantial building. This Bill will render such sites available by giving a secure title to the purchasers under the Act. There are courts and courts in all parts of London from which the owners are reaping large profits, and which they simply wouldn't sell; there are whole plots which would be available for building for the poor, if one owner did not refuse to sell. The Bill enables you (collectively, mind) to take such.

Now, what is our duty, as this power is not vested in a central enlightened individual? Surely it is for us, when we have the Act, to move all to desire to carry it out heartily; not to grudge the taxes it will cost—they will return to us fourfold, I think, and certainly no portion of our income will be better spent—to elect to the vestries, and through them to the Metropolitan Board of Works, or to the Town Councils of our various neighbourhoods, men who will try heartily to make the Bill work; to see that men who care for sanitary reform are elected as medical officers, especially to the Metropolitan Board of Works; to master the provisions of the Bill, and see them enforced; to know the spots where it should come into force; to see that public opinion brings it to bear on them; and to devise suitable schemes of reform for bad neighbourhoods, bearing in mind the special needs of the locality; to lay aside every selfish, nay, every personal, consideration, and with single hearts to desire, and with united will to resolve, that the Act shall improve off the face of the earth the foul buildings unworthy to be tenanted by men.

Now, having long thought all this about the Bill, of course I can't have failed to ask myself what my small efforts are henceforth to be if these my best hopes should be realised for the Bill. Might I then retire and watch over some small group of tenants, as I did in 1866, and leave the larger work to statesmen and town councillors and vestrymen? Why reprint, now of all times, these sketches of tiny schemes and small personal endeavour? The answer comes clearly enough. " There will be no retreat for you yet, even if all outside buildings were put to rights to-morrow. It would simplify your work ; it would not do away with the need of it."

The people's homes are bad, partly because they are badly built and arranged; they are tenfold worse because the tenants' habits and lives are what they are. Transplant them to-morrow to healthy and commodious homes, and they would pollute and destroy them. There needs, and will need for some time, a reformatory work which will demand that loving zeal of individuals which cannot be had for money, and cannot be legislated for by Parliament. The heart of the English nation will supply it—individual, reverent, firm, and wise. It may and should be organised, but cannot be created.

The following papers show a little what is needed in these courts, to help the inhabitants to be fit for far better ones; and, whether in new buildings or in old, some such teaching will be needed among the lowest classes, till they have learnt to be other than they are. The need of voluntary work, the absolute necessity of its being organised, is dealt with in one of the following papers ; the way in which official bodies, such as the Board of Guardians, can make use of it when once organised, is definitely described in the Report to the Local Government Board of 1874.

In the management of the houses, and in that of the districts described in the following papers, it will be noticed that a visitor is set over a small court or block of buildings, and that she is asked to do the work there, whether it be collecting rents, reporting to Guardians, visiting for the School Board, collection of savings, or any other requisite duty, yet that the personal influence which she exercises is not prominently brought before herself or the poor. Thus it has seemed to me that if in a given district any of this definite work becomes gradually unnecessary—as, for instance, out-relief from Guardians ought to do—the supervision would die down, and give place insensibly to the simple intercourse with one another that seems natural to neighbours. But this is looking forward into future years.

One glance back, and I have done. The conduct of this work and its extension have been for some years in my hands, and those of newer friends. I would not for a moment under-value their help ; and it matters little to the public who does a thing, so that it is the right thing to do ; but it matters some-what to anyone who gets an undue share of notice from the success of a work, which, small as it is, has grown far beyond her faintest dreams, to remind the public of one to whom it owes its realisation. This undertaking may be estimated very variously; but anyone who thinks it worth notice should remember distinctly that it might have remained always a mere vision of what I should like to have done, powerless for good, had it not been for the perception of Mr. Ruskin, who alone believed the scheme could be worked, and for his generosity in giving freely and fully all the money spent in the first two courts. It is true it has paid him since—quite true ;

but he risked upwards of £3,000 in the experiment, when not many men would have trusted that the undertaking would succeed. And, moreover, while he assured me that his money was entirely, fully, and freely given for the good of the cause, and if it was sunk, would never be regretted by him, yet he foretold that the work would spread if 1 could make it pay, and urged me therefore to try—a foresight and practical wisdom far beyond mine at the time. I remember well smiling supreme amazement, and saying, "Who will ever hear or know? The important thing is to make it a good thing, realising, as far as may be, your ideal and mine."   But, happily for the scheme, I had gratitude and obedience enough to try heartily to fulfil his ideal on this point; succeeded, and in succeeding learnt how much better a footing the self-supporting one was for the tenants, as well as how right he had been as to the extension of the work itself.

May, 1875.

PREFACE TO SECOND EDITION.

AT this time all words about the homes of the London Poor seem valueless, unless they have a practical bearing. The whole nation is asking what can be done to improve them. It appears to be generally known that the Artisans' Dwellings Act has been costly, and it is of no practical importance to the main subject now whether or not a large part of this cost might have been saved. The expenditure would have been less reluctantly made had the poor been provided for. It is true that large numbers of unsanitary houses have been cleared away. It is true that hundreds of healthy dwellings for working people have been erected. But it is pretty well recognised that few families below that of the artisan class have been accommodated on the sites which have been cleared. The immediate question is (and it is one which imperatively needs to be answered before the last of these sites are sold), how is a lower class to be reached?

The difficulty of dealing with this class is twofold. First, that of management. Second, that of finance.

I say very deliberately that the management is the greater of the two difficulties. How it can be met by the watchful and wise helpfulness of volunteers the following pages show.

Since they were written the work has developed much. Many courts have been purchased and put under volunteer supervision. There is now a larger group of these workers, more are coming forward to be trained, and I cannot help hoping that the day may not be far distant when those who wish to have buildings thus managed may be able to turn to us for help, and that we may be able to accede to their request to a greater degree than we have hitherto done.

The financial difficulty is however the principal one before the public mind just now. I suppose care and economy are more easily practised by individuals than by public bodies. My balance sheets show results which differ considerably from those ordinarily quoted. They relate to houses new and old which have been under my care for many years, and also to recent buildings. I, therefore, do not consider the financial problem nearly so hopeless as it is believed to be. But the strictest economy is needed in building and in management, if dwellings for the poor are to pay.

But even if we accept the higher estimates ordinarily given, they show us that there are two kinds of families of the poorest class, which can be at once accommodated at rents which will yield a fair percentage, if the plans of the blocks built are modified so as to suit their requirements. These families form *a very large number indeed* of those about whom so earnest a cry of dissatisfaction with present dwellings has arisen.

They are :

1st. The small families of unskilled labourers who require good-sized single rooms.

2nd. The larger families of unskilled labourers who have one or two children old enough to work, and who can afford to take a second or even a third room, but whose wages do not allow of their paying for the more elaborate appliances provided in tenements intended for artisans.

To meet the needs of these two classes good-sized single rooms should be built. So far as I know, the single rooms in model dwellings are usually built for one person only, and are quite unsuitable for the thousands of small poor families who want one large room, who indeed prefer it to two small ones. It is not only less costly, but they can see their friends more comfortably, and they themselves feel less cramped. I speak from experience when I say that I know numbers of the prettiest, happiest little homes, which consist of a single room.

Near to these single rooms, but separable from them, smaller ones should be built which could be let with them, whenever wages, or the standard of comfort, rose. There are many tenants who can be induced by a little gentle pressure and encouragement to spend a rather larger proportion than they now do in rent, but who still require the simplest appliances and cheapest rooms compatible with health.

By accommodating these two classes the crowding in existing houses would be diminished.

It would be impossible here to explain details of plan or price, but there are buildings which I could show to anyone interested in the subject which would exemplify how I should propose to build. They are simpler in construction, cheaper in cost than most of those ordinarily built, yet they provide all that is essential to health and even to comfort.

My experience in building and in management is now considerable, and I have no hesitation in saying, that if a site were handed over to me at the price which has hitherto been paid to the Metropolitan Board for those cleared under the Artisans' Dwellings Act, I would engage to house upon it under thoroughly healthy conditions, at rents which they could pay, and which would yield fair interest on capital, a very large proportion of the very poor.   It should be added, that though the houses under my care are managed by volunteers, the ordinary percentage for collection of rents is always charged to the owners, in order that the undertaking may be on a thoroughly sound financial footing, an arrangement which I feel is due to the dignified independence which I hope all my tenants feel in the sense that they are really paying for their own home. This arrangement also gives me the certainty that the plan has the power of growth.

November, 1883.

HOMES OF THE LONDON POOR.

I.

COTTAGE PROPERTY IN LONDON.*

THE subject of dwellings for the poor is attracting so much attention, that an account of a small attempt to improve them may be interesting to many readers, especially as the plan adopted is one which has answered pecuniarily, and which, while it might be undertaken by private individuals without much risk, would bring them into close and healthy communication with their hard-working neighbours.

Two years ago I first had an opportunity of carrying out the plan I had long contemplated, that of obtaining possession of houses to be let in weekly tenements to the poor. That the spiritual elevation of a large class depended to a considerable extent on sanitary reform was, I considered, proved; but I was equally certain that sanitary improvement itself depended upon educational work among grown-up people; that they must be urged to rouse themselves from the lethargy and indolent habits into which they have fallen, and freed from all that hinders them from doing so. I further believed that any lady who would help them to obtain things, the need of which they felt themselves, and would sympathise with them in their desire for such, would soon find them eager to learn her view of what was best for them; that whether this was so or not, her duty was to keep alive their own best hopes and intentions, which come at rare intervals, but fade too often for want of encouragement. I desired to be in a condition to free a few poor people from the tyranny and influence of a low class of

* *Fortnightly Review*, November, 1866.

landlords and landladies; from the corrupting effect of continual forced communication with very degraded fellow-lodgers; from the heavy incubus of accumulated dirt : that so the never-dying hope which I find characteristic of the poor might have leave to spring, and with it such energy as might help them to help themselves.   I had not great ideas of what must be done for them, my strongest endeavours were to be used to rouse habits of industry and effort, without which they must finally sink—with which they might render themselves independent of me, except as a friend and leader.   The plan was one which depended on just governing more than on helping. The first point was to secure such power as would enable me to insist on some essential sanitary arrangements.

I laid the plan before Mr. Ruskin, who entered into it most warmly.   He at once came forward with all the money necessary, and took the whole risk of the undertaking upon himself.   He showed me, however, that it would be far more useful if it could be made to pay ; that a working man ought to be able to pay for his own house ; that the outlay upon it ought, therefore, to yield a fair percentage on the capital invested.   Thus empowered and directed, I purchased three houses in my own immediate neighbourhood.   They were leasehold, subject to a small ground-rent.   The unexpired term of the lease was for fifty-six years ; this we purchased for £750.   We spent £78 additional in making a large room at the back of my own house where I could meet the tenants from time to time.   The plan has now been in operation about a year and a half; the financial result is that the scheme has paid five per cent. interest on all the capital, has repaid £48 of the capital ; sets of two rooms have been let for little more than the rent of one, the houses have been kept in repair, all expenses have been met for taxes, ground-rent, and insurance. In this case there is no expense for collecting rents, as I do it myself, finding it most important work ; but in all the estimates I put aside the usual percentage for it, in case hereafter I may require help, and also to prove practically that it can be afforded in other cases.   It should be observed that well-built houses were chosen, but they were in a dreadful state of dirt and neglect.   The repairs required were mainly of a superficial and slight character : slight in regard to expense—vital as to health and comfort.   The place swarmed with vermin ; the papers, black with dirt, hung in long strips from the walls ; the drains were stopped, the water supply out of order.   All these things were put in order, but no new appliances of any kind were added, as we had determined that our tenants should wait for these until they had proved themselves capable of taking care of them. A regular sum is set aside for repairs, and this is equally divided between the three houses; if any of it remains, after breakage and damage have been repaired, at the end of the quarter each tenant decides in turn in what way the surplus shall be spent, so as to add to the comfort of the house. This plan has worked admirably; the loss from carelessness has decreased to an amazing extent, and the lodgers prize the little comforts which they have waited for, and seem in a measure to have earned by their care, much more than those bought with more lavish expenditure. The bad debts during the whole time that the plan has been in operation have only amounted to £2 11s. 3d. Extreme punctuality and diligence in collecting rents, and a strict determination that they shall be paid regularly, have accomplished this; as a proof of which it is curious to observe that £1 3s. 3d. of the bad debts accumulated during two months that I was away in the country. I have tried to remember, when it seemed hardest, that the fulfilment of their duties was the best education for the tenants in every way. It has given them a dignity and glad feeling of honourable behaviour which has much more than compensated for the apparent harshness of the rule.

Nothing has impressed me more than the people's perception of an underlying current of sympathy through all dealings that have seemed harsh. Somehow, love and care have made themselves felt. It is also wonderful that they should prize as they do the evenness of the law that is over them. They are accustomed to alternate violence of passion and toleration of vice. They expected a greater toleration, ignorant indulgence, and frequent almsgiving, but in spite of this have recognised as a blessing a rule which is very strict, but the demands of which they know, and a government that is true in word and deed. The plan of substituting a lady for a resident landlady of the same class as her tenants is not wholly gain. The lady will probably have subtler sympathy and clearer comprehension of their needs, but she cannot give the same minute supervision that a resident landlady can. Unhappily, the advantage of such a change is, however, at present unquestionable. The influence of the majority of the lower class of people who sub-let to the poor is almost wholly injurious. That tenants should be given up to the dominion of those whose word is given and broken almost as a matter of course, whose habits and standards are very low, whose passions are violent, who have neither large hope nor clear sight, nor even sympathy, is very sad.   It seems to me that a greater power is in the hands of landlords and landladies than of school-teachers—power either of life or death, physical and spiritual.   It is not an unimportant question who shall wield it.   There are dreadful instances in which sin is really tolerated and shared; where the lodger who will drink most with his landlord is most favoured, and many a debt overlooked, to compensate for which the price of rooms is raised; and thus the steady and sober pay more rent to make up for losses caused by the unprincipled.   But take this as an example of entirely careless rule: The owner of some cottage property in London, a small undertaker by trade, living some little distance from his property, and for the most part confining his dealings with it to a somewhat fruitless endeavour to collect the rents on a Sunday morning, in discussing the value of the property with me, said very straightforwardly, " Yes, miss ; of course there are plenty of bad debts.   It's not the rents I look to, but the deaths I get out of the houses."   The man didn't mean for a moment that he knew that the state of the houses brought him a plentiful harvest of deaths, though I knew it and heard the truth ringing with awful irony through his words; but he did mean that his entire thought was of his profits— that those dependent souls and bodies were to him as nothing. Consider under such a rule what deadly quarrels spring up and deepen and widen between families compelled to live very near one another, to use many things in common, whose uneducated minds brood over and over the same slight offences, when there is no one either compulsorily to separate them, or to say some soothing word of reconciliation before the quarrel grows too serious.   I have received a letter from an Irish tenant actually boasting that he " would have taken a more manly way of settling a dispute," but that his neighbour " showed the white feather and retired."   I have seen that man's whole face light up and break into a smile when I suggested that a little willing kindness would be a more manly way still.   And I have known him and his aunt, though boiling over with rage all the time, use steady self-control in not quarrelling for a whole month, because they knew it would spoil my holiday !   Finally, they shook hands and made peace, and lived in peace many months, and, indeed, are living so now.

I could have formed no idea of the docility of the people,

nor of their gratitude for small things. They are easily governed by firmness, which they respect much. I have always made a point of carefully recognising their own rights ; but if a strong conviction is clearly expressed they readily adopt it, and they often accept a different idea from any they have previously desired, if it is set before them. One tenant —a silent, strong, uncringing woman, living with her seven children and her husband in one room—was certain " there were many things she could get for the children to eat which would do them more good than another room." I was perfectly silent. A half-pleading, half-asserting voice said : " Don't you see I'm right, miss?" " No," I said ; " indeed I do not. I have been brought up to know the value of abundant good air ; but of course you must do as you think best—only I am sorry." Not a word more passed ; but in a few weeks a second room was again to let, and the woman volunteered : " She thought she'd better strive to get the rent ; good air was very important, wasn't it?" Again : a man wouldn't send his children to school. Dirty, neglected, and unhappy, they destroyed many things in the house. I urged, to no purpose, that they should be sent. At last I gave him notice to leave because he refused to send them, and because he had taken three children to sleep in the room I had let for his own family only. The man was both angry and obstinate. I quietly went on with proceedings for getting rid of him. He knew I meant what I said, and he requested an interview. He owed no rent, he urged. " No," I replied, "you know what a point I make of that; but it isn't quite the only thing I insist on. I cannot allow anything so wrong as this neglect of the children and overcrowding to continue where I have the power to prevent it." He "knew what it was just this year to fuss about the cholera, and then nobody'd care how many slep in a room ; but he wasn't a coward to be frightened at the cholera, not he ! And as to being bound, he wouldn't be bound—no, not to his own master that paid him wage ; and it wasn't likely he would to me, when he paid rent reg'lar. The room was his ; he took it, and if he paid rent he could do as he liked in it." " Very well," I said ; " and the house is mine; I take it, and I must do what I think right in it ; and I say that most landladies won't take in children at all, and we all know it is a good deal of loss and trouble ; but I will risk these gladly if you will do what you can to teach the children to be good, and careful, and industrious ; and if not, you know the rule, and you must go. If you prefer liberty, and dirt,

and mess, take them ; but if you choose to agree to live under
as good a rule as I can make it, you can stay. You have your
choice." Put in the light of a bargain the man was willing
enough. Well, he'd not " do anything contrairy, without
telling me, about lodgers ; and as to the children, he thought
he could turn himself, and send them a bit, now his work was
better."

With the great want of rooms there is in this neighbourhood, it did not seem right to expel families, however large,
inhabiting one room. Whenever from any cause a room was
vacant, and a large family occupied an adjoining one, I have
endeavoured to induce them to rent the two. To incoming
tenants I do not let what seems decidedly insufficient accommodation. We have been able to let two rooms for four
shillings and sixpence, whereas the tenants were in many cases
paying four shillings for one. At first they considered it quite
an unnecessary expenditure to pay more rent for a second
room, however small the additional sum might be. They have
gradually learnt to feel the comfort of having two rooms, and
pay willingly for them.

The pecuniary success of the plan has been due to two
causes. First, to the absence of middlemen ; and secondly,
to great strictness about punctual payment of rent. At this
moment not one tenant in any of the houses owes any rent,
and during the whole time, as I have said, the bad debts have
been exceedingly small. The law respecting such tenancies
seems very simple, and when once the method of proceeding is
understood, the whole business is easily managed ; and I must
say most seriously that I believe it to be better to pay legal
expenses for getting rid of tenants than to lose by arrears of
rent—better for the whole tone of the households, kinder to
the tenants. The rule should be clearly understood, and the
people will respect themselves for having obeyed it. The
commencement of proceedings which are known to be genuine,
and not a mere threat, is usually sufficient to obtain payment
of arrears : in one case only has an ejectment for rent been
necessary. The great want of rooms gives the possessors of
such property immense power over their lodgers. Let them
see to it that they use it righteously. The fluctuations of work
cause to respectable tenants the main difficulties in paying
their rent. I have tried to help them in two ways. First, by
inducing them to save : this they have done steadily, and each
autumn has found them with a small fund accumulated, which
has enabled them to meet the difficulties of the time when

families are out of town. In the second place, I have done what I could to employ my tenants in slack seasons. I carefully set aside any work they can do for times of scarcity, and I try so to equalise in this small circle the irregularity of work, which must be more or less pernicious, and which the childishness of the poor makes doubly so. They have strangely little power of looking forward; a result is to them as nothing if it will rot be perceptible till next quarter! This is very curious to me, especially as seen in connection with that large hope to which I have alluded, and which often makes me think that if I could I would carve over the houses the motto, "Spem, etiam illi habent, quibus nihil aliud restat."

Another beautiful trait in their character is their trust; it has been quite marvellous to find how great and how ready this is. In no single case have I met with suspicion or with anything but entire confidence.

It is needless to say that there have been many minor difficulties and disappointments. Each separate person who has failed to rise and meet the help that would have been so gladly given has been a distinct loss to me; for somehow the sense of relation to them has been a very real one, and a feeling of interest and responsibility has been very strong, even where there was least that was lovely or lovable in the particular character. When they have not had sufficient energy or self-control to choose the sometimes hard path that has seemed the only right one, it would have been hard to part from them, except for a hope that others would be able to lead them where I have failed.

Two distinct kinds of work depend entirely on one another if they are to bear their full fruit. There is, firstly, the simple fulfilment of a landlady's bounden duties, and uniform demand of the fulfilment of those of the tenants. We have felt ourselves bound by laws which must be obeyed, however hard obedience might often be. Then, secondly, there is the individual friendship which has grown up from intimate knowledge, and from a sense of dependence and protection. Such knowledge gives power to see the real position of families; to suggest in time the inevitable result of certain habits; to urge such measures as shall secure the education of the children and their establishment in life; to keep alive the germs of energy; to waken the gentler thought; to refuse resolutely to give any help but such as rouses self-help; to cherish the smallest lingering gleam of self-respect; and, finally, to be near with strong help should the hour of trial fall suddenly and heavily, and to give it with the hand and heart of a real old friend, who has filled many relations besides that of almsgiver, who has long ago given far more than material help, and has thus earned the right to give this lesser help even to the most independent spirits.

The relation will finally depend on the human spirits hat enter into it; like all others, it may be pernicious or helpful. It is simply a large field of labour where the labourers are few. It has this advantage over many beneficent works—that it calls out a sense of duty, and demands energetic right-doing among the poor themselves, and so purifies and stimuates them.

If any of my poorer friends chance to see this, I hope they will not think I have spoken too exclusively of what we can do for them. I have dwelt on this side of the question because it is the one we are mainly bound to consider; it is for then to think how they can help us. But I must add in gratitude that I have much to thank them for. Their energy and hope amid overwhelming difficulties have made me ashamed of my own laziness and despair. I have seen the inevitable result of faults and omissions of mine that I had never sufficiently weighed. Their patience and thankfulness are a glad cause of admiration to me continually. I trust that our relation to one another may grow better and nearer for many years.

November 1st, 1866.

II.

FOUR YEARS' MANAGEMENT OF A LONDON COURT.*

FURTHER organisation in our mode of dealing with the poor is now generally agreed to be necessary; but there is another truth less dwelt upon, yet on the due recognition of which success equally depends. I feel most deeply that the disciplining of our immense poor population must be effected by individual influence; and that this power can change it from a mob of paupers and semi-paupers into a body of self-dependent workers. It is my opinion, further, that although such influence may be brought to bear upon them in very various ways, it may be exercised in a very remarkable manner by persons undertaking the oversight and management of such houses as the poor habitually lodge in. In support of this opinion I subjoin an account of what has been actually achieved in two very poor courts in London.

About four years ago I was put in possession of three houses in one of the worst courts in Marylebone. Six other houses were bought subsequently. All were crowded with inmates. The first thing to be done was to put them in decent tenantable order. The set last purchased was a row of cottages facing a bit of desolate ground, occupied with wretched, dilapidated cow-sheds, manure heaps, old timber, and rubbish of every description. The houses were in a most deplorable condition—the plaster was dropping from the walls; on one staircase a pail was placed to catch the rain that fell through the roof. All the staircases were perfectly dark; the banisters were gone, having been burnt as firewood by tenants. The grates, with large holes in them, were falling forward into the rooms.

* *Macmillan's Magazine*, July, 1869.

The wash-house, full of lumber belonging to the landlord, was locked up ; thus the inhabitants had to wash clothes, as well as to cook, eat, and sleep in their small rooms. The dust-bin, standing in the front of the houses, was accessible to the whole neighbourhood, and boys often dragged from it quantities of unseemly objects and spread them over the court. The state of the drainage was in keeping with everything else. The pavement of the back-yard was all broken up, and great puddles stood in it, so that the damp crept up the outer walls. One large but dirty water-butt received the water laid on for the houses ; it leaked, and for such as did not fill their jugs when the water came in, or who had no jugs to fill, there was no water. The former landlord's reply to one of the tenants who asked him to have an iron hoop put round the butt to prevent leakage, was, that "if he didn't like it" (*i.e.* things as they were) "he might leave." The man to whom this was spoken —by far the best tenant in the place—is now with us, and often gives his spare time to making his room more comfortable, knowing that he will be retained if he behaves well.

This landlord was a tradesman in a small way of business —not a cruel man, except in so far as variableness of dealing is cruelty ; but he was a man without capital to spend on improvements, and lost an immense percentage of his rent by bad debts. I went over the houses with him the last day he collected his rents there, that he might introduce me to the people as the owner of the property. He took a man with him, whom, as he confided to me, he wished to pass off upon the people as a broker.* It was evident that, whether they saw through this deceit or not, they had no experience which led them to believe he intended to carry into effect the threats he uttered. The arrears of rent were enormous. I had been informed that the honest habitually pay for the dishonest, the owner relying upon their payments to compensate for all losses ; but I was amazed to find to what an extent this was the case. Six, seven, or eight weeks' rent was due from most tenants, and in some cases very much more ; whereas, since I took possession of the houses (of which I collect the rents each week myself) I have *never* allowed a second week's rent to become due.

I think no one who has not experienced it can fully realise the almost awed sense of joy with which one enters upon such a possession as that above described, conscious of having the

* The ultimate step taken to enforce payment of rent is to send in a broker to distrain.

power to set it, even partially, in order. Hopes, indeed, there are which one dares scarcely hope; but at once one has power to say, "Break out a window there in that dark corner; let God's light and air in;" or, "Trap that foul drain, and shut the poisonous miasma out;" and one has moral power to say, by deeds which speak louder than words, "Where God gives me authority, this, which you in your own hearts know to be wrong, shall not go on. I would not set my conviction, however strong it might be, against your judgment of right; but when you are doing what I know your own conscience condemns, I, now that I have the power, will enforce right; but first I will try whether I cannot *lead* you, yourselves, to arise and cast out the sin—helping your wavering and sorely tried will by mine, which is untempted."

As soon as I entered into possession, each family had an opportunity of doing better: those who would not pay, or who led clearly immoral lives, were ejected. The rooms they vacated were cleansed; the tenants who showed signs of improvement moved into them, and thus, in turn, an opportunity was obtained for having each room distempered and painted. The drains were put in order, a large slate cistern was fixed, the wash-house was cleared of its lumber, and thrown open on stated days to each tenant in turn. The roof, the plaster, the woodwork were repaired; the staircase-walls were distempered; new grates were fixed; the layers of paper and rag (black with age) were torn from the windows, and glass was put in; out of 192 panes, only 8 were unbroken. The yard and footpath were paved.

The rooms, as a rule, were re-let at the same prices at which they had been let before; but tenants with large families were counselled to take two rooms, and for these much less was charged than if let singly: this plan I continue to pursue. In-coming tenants are not allowed to take a decidedly insufficient quantity of room, and no sub-letting is permitted. The elder girls are employed three times a week in scrubbing the passages in the houses, for the cleaning of which the landlady is responsible. For this work they are paid, and by it they learn habits of cleanliness. It is, of course, within the authority of the landlady also to insist on cleanliness of wash-houses, yards, staircases, and staircase-windows; and even to remonstrate concerning the rooms themselves if they are habitually dirty.

The pecuniary result has been very satisfactory. Five **per** cent. interest has been paid on all the capital invested. **A** fund for the repayment of capital is accumulating. A liberal allowance has been made for repairs ; and here I may speak of the means adopted for making the tenants careful about breakage and waste. The sum allowed yearly for repairs is fixed for each house, and if it has not all been spent in restoring and replacing, the surplus is used for providing such additional appliances as the tenants themselves desire. It is therefore to their interest to keep the expenditure for repairs as low as possible ; and instead of committing the wanton damage common among tenants of their class, they are careful to avoid injury, and very helpful in finding economical methods of restoring what is broken or worn out, often doing little repairs of their own accord.

From the proceeds of the rent, also, interest has been paid on the capital spent in building a large room where the tenants can assemble. Classes are held there—for boys, twice weekly ; for girls, once ; a singing class has just been established. A large work-class for married women and elder girls meets once a week. A glad sight it is—the large room filled with the eager, merry faces of the girls, from which those of the older, careworn women catch a reflected light. It is a good time for quiet talk with them as we work, and many a neighbourly feeling is called out among the women as they sit together on the same bench, lend one another cotton or needles, are served by the same hand, and look to the same person for direction. The babies are a great bond of union : I have known the very women who not long before had been literally fighting, sit at the work-class busily and earnestly comparing notes of their babies' respective history. That a consciousness of corporate life is developed in them is shown by the not infrequent use of the expression " One of us."

Among the arrangements conducive to comfort and health, I may mention that instead of the clothes being hung, as formerly, out of front windows down against the wall, where they could not be properly purified, the piece of ground in front of the houses is used as a drying-ground during school hours. The same place is appropriated as a playground, not only for my younger tenants, but for the children of the neighbouring courts. It is a space walled round, where they can play in safety. Hitherto, games at trap, bat and ball, swinging, skipping, and singing a few Kinder-Garten songs with movements in unison, have been the main diversions. But I have just established drill for the boys, and a drum and fife band. Unhappily, the mere business connected with the working of the houses has occupied so much time, that the playground has been somewhat neglected; yet it is a most important part of the work. The evils of the streets and courts are too evident to need explanation. In the playground are gathered together children habitually dirty, quarrelsome, and violent. They come wholly ignorant of games, and have hardly self-control enough to play at any which have an object or require effort. Mere senseless, endless repetition is at best their diversion. Often the games are only repetitions of questionable sentences. For instance, what is to be said of a game the whole of which consists in singing, " Here comes my father all down the hill, all down the hill" (over and over again), and replying, "We won't get up for his ugly face—ugly face" (repeated *ad libitum*)? Then come the mother, the sister, the brother, to whom the same words are addressed. Finally the lover comes, to whom the greeting is, " We will get up for his pretty face." This was, perhaps, the best game the children knew, yet, in as far as it had any meaning or influence, it must be bad. Compare it, or the wild, lawless fighting or gambling, with a game at trap, arranged with ordered companions, definite object, and progressive skill. The moral influence depends, however, on having ladies who will go to the playground, teach games, act as umpires, know and care for the children. These I hope to find more and more. Until now, except at rare intervals, the playground has been mainly useful for the fresh air it affords to the children who are huddled together by night in small rooms, in the surrounding courts. The more respectable parents keep them indoors, even in the daytime, after school-hours, to prevent their meeting with bad companions.

Mr. Ruskin, to whom the whole undertaking owes its existence, has had trees planted in the playground, and creepers against the houses. In May, we have a May-pole or a throne covered with flowers for the May-queen and her attendants. The sweet luxuriance of the spring flowers is more enjoyed in that court than would readily be believed. Some months after the first festival the children were seen sticking a few faded flowers into a crevice in the wall, saying they wanted to make it "like it was the day we had the May-pole."

I have tried, as far as opportunity has permitted, to develop the love of beauty among my tenants. The poor of London need joy and beauty in their lives. There is no more true and eternal law to be recognised about them than that which Mr. Dickens shows in " Hard Times "—the fact that every man

has an imagination which needs development and satisfaction·
Mr. Slearey's speech, "People mutht be amoothed, Thquire,"
is often recalled to my mind in dealing with the poor. They
work hard ; their lives are monotonous ; they seek low places
of amusement ; they break out into lawless "sprees." Almost
all amusements—singing, dancing, acting, expeditions into the
country, eating and drinking—are liable to abuse ; no rules are
subtle enough to prevent their leading to harm. But if a lady
can know the individuals, and ask them as her invited guests
to any of these, an innate sense of honour and respect pre-
serves the tone through the whole company. Indeed, there
can hardly be a more proudly thankful moment than that,
when we see these many people, to whom life is dull and full
of anxiety, gathered together around us for holy, happy Christmas festivities, or going out to some fair and quiet spot in the
bright summer time, bound to one another by the sense of
common relationship, preserved unconsciously from wrong by
the presence of those whom they love and who love them.
Such intervals of bright joy are easily arranged by friends for
friends ; but if strangers are invited *en masse*, it is difficult to
keep any of these recreations innocent.

All these ways of meeting are invaluable as binding us
together ; still they would avail little were it not for the work by
which we are connected, for the individual care each member
of the little circle receives. Week by week, when the rents are
collected, an opportunity of seeing each family separately
occurs. There are a multitude of matters to attend to. First,
there is the mere outside business—rent to be received, requests
from the tenant respecting repairs to be considered ; sometimes decisions touching the behaviour of other tenants to be
made, sometimes rebukes for untidiness to be administered.
Then come the sad or joyful remarks about health or work, the
little histories of the week. Sometimes grave questions arise
about important changes in the life of the family—shall a
daughter go to service ? or shall the sick child be sent to a
hospital ? etc.

Sometimes violent quarrels must be allayed. Much may
be done in this way, so ready is the response in these affectionate natures to those whom they trust and love. For
instance : two women among my tenants fought ; one received
a dreadful kick, the other had hair torn from her head. They
were parted by a lad who lived in the house. The women
occupied adjoining rooms, they met in the passages, they
used the same yard and wash-house, endless were the oppor-

tunities of collision while they were engaged with each other. For ten days I saw them repeatedly; I could in no way reconcile them—words of rage and recrimination were all that they uttered; while the hair, which had been carefully preserved by the victim, was continually exhibited to me as a sufficient justification for lasting anger. One was a cold, hard, self-satisfied, well-to-do woman; the other a nervous, affectionate, passionate, very poor Irish-woman. Now it happened that in speaking to the latter one evening, I mentioned my own grief at the quarrel; a look of extreme pain came over her face—it was a new idea to her that I should care. That, and no sense of the wrong of indulging an evil passion, touched her. The warm-hearted creature at once promised to shake hands with her adversary; but she had already taken out a summons against the other for assault, and did not consider she could afford to make up the quarrel because it implied losing the two shillings the summons had cost. I told her the loss was a mere nothing to her if weighed in the balance with peace, but that I would willingly pay it. It only needed that one of the combatants should make the first step towards reconciliation for the other—who, indeed, rather dreaded answering the summons—to meet her half-way. They are good neighbours now of some months' standing. A little speech, which shows the character of the Irishwoman, is worth recording. Acknowledging to me that she was very passionate, she said : " My husband never takes my part when I'm in my tanthrums, and I'm that mad with him; but, bless you, I love him all the better afterwards; he knows well enough it would only make me worse." I may here observe that the above-mentioned two shillings is the only money I ever had to give to either woman. It is on such infinitesimally small actions that the success of the whole work rests.

My tenants are mostly of a class far below that of mechanics. They are, indeed, of the very poor. And yet, although the gifts they have received have been next to nothing, none of the families who have passed under my care during the whole four years have continued in what is called " distress," except such as have been unwilling to exert themselves. Those who will not exert the necessary self-control cannot avail themselves of the means of livelihood held out to them. But, for those who are willing, some small assistance in the form of work has, from time to time, been provided—not much, but sufficient to keep them from want or despair. The following will serve as an instance of the sort of help given, and its proportion to the results.

Alice, a single woman, of perhaps fifty-five years, lodged with a man and his wife—the three in one room—just before I obtained full possession of the houses. Alice, not being able to pay her rent, was turned into the street, where Mrs. S. —my playground superintendent—met her, crying dreadfully.

It was Saturday, and I had left town till Monday. Alice had neither furniture to pawn nor friends to help her; the workhouse alone lay before her. Mrs. S. knew that I esteemed her as a sober, respectable, industrious woman, and therefore she ventured to express to Alice's landlord the belief that I would not let him lose money if he would let her go back to her lodging till Monday, when I should return home, thus risking for me a possible loss of fourpence—not very ruinous to me, and a sum not impossible for Alice to repay in the future.

I gave Alice two days' needlework, then found her employment in tending a bedridden cottager in the country, whose daughter (in service) paid for the nursing. Five weeks she was there, working and saving her money. On her return I lent her what more she required to buy furniture, and then she took a little room direct from me. Too blind to do much household work, but able to sew almost mechanically, she just earns her daily bread by making sailors' shirts, but her little home is her own, and she loves it dearly; and, having tided over that time of trial, Alice can live—has paid all her debts too, and is more grateful than she would have been for many gifts.

At one time I had a room to let which was ninepence a week cheaper than the one she occupied. I proposed to her to take it; it had, however, a different aspect, getting less of the southern and western sunlight. Alice hesitated long, and asked *me* to decide, which I declined to do; for, as I told her, her moving would suit my arrangements rather better. She, hearing that, wished to move; but I begged her to make her decision wholly irrespective of my plans. At last she said, very wistfully, "Well, you see, miss, it's between ninepence and the sun." Sadly enough, ninepence had to outweigh the sun.

My tenants are, of course, encouraged to save their money. It should, however, be remarked that I have never succeeded in getting them to save for old age. The utmost I have achieved is that they lay by sufficient either to pay rent in times of scarcity, to provide clothes for girls going to service, or boots, or furniture, or even to avail themselves of opportunities of advancement which must be closed to them if they had not a little reserve fund to meet expenses of the change.

One great advantage arising from the management of the houses is that they form a test-place, in which people may prove themselves worthy of higher situations. Not a few of the tenants have been persons who had sunk below the stratum where once they were known, and some of these, simply by proving their character, have been enabled to regain their former stations. One man, twenty years ago, had been a gentleman's servant, had saved money, gone into business, married, failed, and then found himself out of the groove of work. When I made his acquaintance he was earning a miserable pittance for his wife and seven unhealthy children, and all the nine souls were suffering and sinking unknown. After watching and proving him for three years, I was able to recommend him to a gentleman in the country, where now the whole family are profiting by having six rooms instead of one, fresh air, and regular wages.

But it is far easier to be helpful than to have patience and self-control sufficient, when the times come, for seeing suffering and not relieving it. And yet the main tone of action must be severe. There is much of rebuke and repression needed, although a deep and silent under-current of sympathy and pity may flow beneath. If the rent is not ready, notice to quit must be served. The money is then almost always paid, when the notice is, of course, withdrawn. Besides this inexorable demand for rent (never to be relaxed without entailing cumulative evil on the defaulter, and setting a bad example, too readily followed by others), there must be a perpetual crusade carried on against small evils—very wearing sometimes. It is necessary to believe that in thus setting in order certain spots on God's earth, still more in presenting to a few of His children a somewhat higher standard of right, we are doing His work, and that He will not permit us to lose sight of His large laws, but will rather make them evident to us through the small details.

The resolution to watch pain which cannot be radically relieved except by the sufferer himself is most difficult to maintain. Yet it is wholly necessary in certain cases not to help. Where a man persistently refuses to exert himself, external help is worse than useless. By withholding gifts we say to him in action more mournful than words: "You will not do better."

I was ready—I will be ready whenever you come to yourself; but until then you must pursue your own course." This attitude has often to be taken; but it usually proves a summons to a more energetic spirit, producing nobler effort in great matters, just as the notice to quit arouses resolution and self-denial in pecuniary concerns.

Coming together so much as we do for business with mutual duties, for recreation with common joy, each separate want or fault having been dealt with as it arose, it will be readily understood that in such a crisis as that which periodically occurs in the East-end of London, instead of being unprepared, I feel myself somewhat like an officer at the head of a well-controlled little regiment, or, more accurately, like a country proprietor with a moderate number of well-ordered tenants.

For, firstly, my people are numbered; not merely counted, but known, man, woman, and child. I have seen their self-denying efforts to pay rent in time of trouble, or their reckless extravagance in seasons of abundance; their patient labour, or their failure to use the self-control necessary to the performance of the more remunerative kinds of work; their efforts to keep their children at school, or their selfish, lazy way of living on their children's earnings. Could anyone, going suddenly among even so small a number as these thirty-four families—however much penetration and zeal he might possess—know so accurately as I what kind of assistance would be really helpful, and not corrupting? And if positive gifts must be resorted to, who can give them with so little pain to the proud spirit, so little risk of undermining the feeble one, as the friend of old standing?—the friend, moreover, who has rigorously exacted the fulfilment of their duty in punctual payment of rent; towards whom, therefore, they might feel that they had done what they could while strength lasted, and need not surely be ashamed to receive a little bread in time of terrible want?

But it ought hardly ever to come to an actual doling out of bread or alms of any kind. During the winter of 1867–68, while the newspapers were ringing with appeals in consequence of the distress prevalent in the metropolis, being on the Continent, and unable to organise more satisfactory schemes of assistance, I wrote to the ladies who were superintending the houses for me, to suggest that a small fund (which had accumulated from the rents, after defraying expenses and paying interest) should be distributed in gifts to any of the families who might be in great poverty. The answer was that there were none requiring such help. Now, how did this come to pass?

Simply through the operation of the various influences above described. The tenants never having been allowed to involve themselves in debt for rent (now and then being supplied with employment to enable them to pay it), they were free from one of the greatest drags upon a poor family, and had, moreover, in times of prosperity been able really to save. It is but too often the case that, even when prosperous times come, working people cannot lay by, because then they have to pay off arrears of rent. The elder girls, too, were either in service or quite ready to go; and so steady, tidy, and respectable as to be able to fill good situations. This was owing, in many cases, to a word or two spoken long before, urging their longer attendance at school, or to their having had a few happy and innocent amusements provided for them, which had satisfied their natural craving for recreation, and had prevented their breaking loose in search of it. Health had been secured by an abundance of air, light, and water. Even among this very lowest class of people, I had found individuals whom I could draft from my lodging-houses into resident situations (transplanting them thus at once into a higher grade), simply because I was able to say, "I know them to be honest, I know them to be clean." Think of what this mere fact of *being known* is to the poor!

You may say, perhaps, "This is very well as far as you and your small knot of tenants are concerned, but how does it help us to deal with the vast masses of poor in our great towns?" I reply, "Are not the great masses made up of many small knots? Are not the great towns divisible into small districts? Are there not people who would gladly come forward to undertake the systematic supervision of some house or houses, if they could get authority from the owner? And why should there not be some way of registering such supervision, so that, bit by bit, as more volunteers should come forward, the whole metropolis might be mapped out, all the blocks fitting in like little bits of mosaic to form one connected whole?"

The success of the plan does not depend entirely upon the houses being the property of the superintendent. I would urge people, if possible, to purchase the houses of which they undertake the charge; but, if they cannot, they may yet do a valuable little bit of work by registering a distinct declaration that they will supervise such and such a house, or row, or street; that if they have to relinquish the work they will say so; that if it becomes too. much for them, they will ask for help; that anyone desiring information about the families dwelling in the houses they manage may apply to them.

It is well known that the societies at work among the poor are so numerous, and labour so independently of each other, that, at present, many sets of people may administer relief to a given family in one day, and perhaps not one go near them again for a long interval; yet each society may be quite systematic in its own field of operation. It seems to me, that though each society might like to go its own way (and, perhaps, to supply wants which the house-overseer might think it best to leave unsupplied), they might at least feel it an advantage to know of a recognised authority, from whom particulars could be learned respecting relief already given, and the history of the families in question.

Any persons accustomed to visit among the poor in a large district would, I believe, when confining themselves to a much smaller one, be led, if not to very unexpected conclusions, at least to very curious problems. In dealing with a large number of cases the urgency is so great one passes over the most difficult questions to work where sight is clear; and one is apt to forget Sissy Jupe's quick sympathetic perception that percentage signifies literally nothing to the friends of the special sufferer, who surely is not worth less than a sparrow. The individual case, if we cared enough for it, would often give us the key to many.

Whoever will limit his gaze to a few persons, and try to solve the problem of their lives—planning, for instance, definitely, how he, even with superior advantages of education, self-control, and knowledge, could bring up a given family on given wages, allowing the smallest amount conceivably sufficient for food, rent, clothes, fuel, and the rest—he may find it in most cases a much more difficult thing than he had ever thought, and sometimes, maybe, an impossibility. It may lead to strange self-questioning about wages. Again, if people will watch carefully the different effect of self-help and of alms, how the latter, like the outdoor relief system under the old Poor-Law, tends to lower wages, and undermines the providence of the poor, it may make them put some searching questions to themselves upon the wisdom of backing up wages with gifts. Then they may begin to consider practically whether in their own small sphere they can form no schemes of help, which shall be life-giving, stimulating hope, energy, foresight, self-denial, and choice of right rather than wrong expenditure.

They may earnestly strive to discover plans of help which shall free them from the oppressive responsibility of deciding whether aid is deserved—a question often complicated inextricably with another, namely, whether at a given moment there is a probability of reformation. All of us have felt the impossibility of deciding either question fairly, yet we have been convinced that gifts coming at the wrong time are often deadly. Earnest workers feel a heavy weight on their hearts and consciences from the conviction that the old command, "Judge not," is a divine one, and yet that the distribution of alms irrespective of character is fatal. These difficulties lead to variable action, which is particularly disastrous with the poor. But there are plans which cultivate the qualities wherein they are habitually wanting, namely, self-control, energy, prudence, and industry; and such plans, if we will do our part, may be ready at any moment for even the least deserving, and for those who have fallen lowest.

Further details as to modes of help must vary infinitely with circumstances and character. But I may mention a few laws which become clearer and clearer to me as I work.

It is best strictly to enforce fulfilment of all such duties as payment of rent, etc.

It is far better to give work than either money or goods.

It is most helpful of all to strengthen by sympathy and counsel the energetic effort which shall bear fruit in time to come.

It is essential to remember that each man has his own view of his life, and must be free to fulfil it; that in many ways he is a far better judge of it than we, as he has lived through and felt what we have only seen. Our work is rather to bring him to the point of considering, and to the spirit of judging rightly, than to consider or judge for him.

The poor of London (as of all large towns) need the development of every power which can open to them noble sources of joy.

III

LANDLORDS AND TENANTS IN LONDON.*

THREE ladies were standing, not long ago, in a poor and dingy court in London, when a group of dirty-faced urchins exclaimed, in a tone, partly of impudence and partly of fun: "What a lot o' landladies this morning!"

The words set me thinking, for I felt that the boys' mirth was excited, not only by the number of landladies (or of ladies acting as such), but also, probably, by the contrast between these ladies and the landladies they usually saw. For the landlady to the London poor is too often a struggling, cheated, much-worried, long-suffering woman; soured by constant dealing with untrustworthy people; embittered by loss; a prey to the worst lodgers, whom she allows to fall into debt, and is afraid to turn out, lest she should lose the amount they owe her; without spirit or education to enable her to devise improvements, or capital to execute them—never able, in short, to use the power given her by her position to bring order into the lives of her tenants: being, indeed, too frequently entirely under their control. There is a numerous class of landladies worse even than this—bullying, violent, passionate, revengeful, and cowardly. They alternately cajole and threaten, but rarely intend to carry out either their promises or their threats. Severe without principle, weakly indulgent towards evil, given to lying and swearing, too covetous to be drunken, yet indulgent to any lodger who will "treat" them; their influence is incalculably mischievous.

Ought this to be the idea suggested by the word "landlady" to the poor of our cities? The old word "landlord" is a proud one to many an English gentleman, who holds

* *Macmillan's Magazine*, October, 1871.

dominion over the neat cottage, with its well-stocked garden; over the comfortable farm-house; over broad, sloping parks, and rich farm-lands. It is a delight to him to keep thus fair the part of the earth over which it has been given him to rule. And, as to his people, he would think it shameful to receive the rents from his well-managed estates in the country, year by year, without some slight recognition of his tenantry—at least on birthdays or at Christmas.

But where are the owners, or lords, or ladies, of most courts like that in which I stood with my two fellow-workers? Who holds dominion there? Who heads the tenants there? If any among the nobly born, or better educated, own them, do they bear the mark of their hands? And if they do *not* own them, might they not do so? There are in those courts as loyal English hearts as ever loved or reverenced the squire in the village, only they have been so forgotten. Dark under the level ground, in kitchens damp with foulest moisture, there they huddle in multitudes, and no one loves or raises them. It must not be thought that the overworked clergymen and missionaries, heroic as they often are, can do all that might be done for them. They count their flock by thousands, and these people want watching one by one. The clergy have no control over these places, nor have they half the power of directing labour to useful ends, which those might have who owned the houses, and were constantly brought into direct contact with the people.

How this relation of landlord and tenant might be established in some of the lowest districts of London, and with what results, I am about to describe by relating what has been done in the last two years in a court in Marylebone. I have already* given an account of my former efforts to establish this relation on a healthy footing in another London court; of the details of my plan of action; and of its success. I am not, therefore, in what follows, putting forth anything new in its main idea, but am simply insisting on principles of the truth of which every day's experience only makes me the more deeply assured, and recounting the history of an attempt to spread those principles to a class still lower than that alluded to in my former paper.

It was near the end of 1869 that I first heard that a good many houses in a court near my own house were to be disposed of. Eventually, in the course of that year, six ten-roomed houses were bought by the Countess of Ducie, and five more

* *Macmillan's Magazine*, July, 1869.

by another lady, and placed partially under my care. I was especially glad to obtain some influence here, as I knew this place to be one of the worst in Marylebone ; its inhabitants were mainly costermongers and small hawkers, and were almost the poorest class of those amongst our population who have any settled home, the next grade below them being vagrants who sleep in common lodging-houses ; and I knew that its moral standing was equally low.   Its reputation had long been familiar to me ; for when unruly and hopeless tenants were sent away from other houses in the district, I had often heard that they had gone to this court, the tone in which it was said implying that they had now sunk to the lowest depths of degradation.   A lawyer friend had also said to me, on hearing that it was proposed to buy houses there, "That court ! why, that is the place one is always noticing in the police reports for its rows."

Yet its outward appearance would not have led a casual observer to guess its real character.   It is not far from Cavendish Square, and daily in the season, scores of carriages, with their gaily-dressed occupants, pass the end of it.   Should such look down it, they would little divine its inner life.   Seen from the outside, and in the daytime, it is a quiet-looking place, the houses a moderate size, and the space between them tolerably wide.   It has no roadway, but is nicely enough paved, and old furniture stands out for sale on the pavement, in front of the few shops.

But if anyone had entered those houses with me two years ago, he would have seen enough to surprise and horrify him. In many of the houses the dustbins were utterly unapproachable, and cabbage-leaves, stale fish, and every sort of dirt were lying in the passages and on the stairs ; in some the back kitchen had been used as a dustbin, but had not been emptied for years, and the dust filtered through into the front kitchens, which were the sole living and sleeping rooms of some families ; in some the kitchen stairs were many inches thick with dirt, which was so hardened that a shovel had to be used to get it off ; in some there was hardly any water to be had ; the wood was eaten and broken away ; windows were smashed ; and the rain was coming through the roofs.   At night it was still worse ; and during the first winter I had to collect the rents chiefly then, as the inhabitants, being principally costermongers, were out nearly all day, and they were afraid to entrust their rent to their neighbours.   It was then that I saw the houses in their most dreadful aspect.   I well remember wet, foggy Monday

nights, when I turned down the dingy court, past the brilliantly-
lighted public-house at the corner, past the old furniture outside the shops, and dived into the dark yawning passage ways.
The front doors stood open day and night, and as I felt my
way down the kitchen-stairs, broken and rounded by the
hardened mud upon them, the foul smells which the heavy
foggy air would not allow to rise met me as I descended, and
the plaster rattled down with a hollow sound as I groped along.
It was truly appalling to think that there were human beings
who lived habitually in such an atmosphere, with such surroundings. Sometimes I had to open the kitchen door myself,
after knocking several times in vain, when a woman, quite
drunk, would be lying on the floor on some black mass which
served as a bed ; sometimes, in answer to my knocks, a half-
drunken man would swear, and thrust the rent-money out to
me through a chink of the door, placing his foot against it, so
as to prevent it from opening wide enough to admit me.
Always it would be shut again without a light being offered to
guide me up the pitch-dark stairs. Such was the court in the
winter of 1869. Truly a wild, lawless, desolate little kingdom
to come to rule over.

On what principles was I to rule these people ? On the
same that I had already tried, and tried with success, in other
places, and which I may sum up as the two following : firstly,
to demand a strict fulfilment of their duties to me—one of the
chief of which would be the punctual payment of rent ; and
secondly, to endeavour to be so unfailingly just and patient,
that they should learn to trust the rule that was over them.

With regard to details, I would make a few improvements
at once—such, for example, as the laying on of water and
repairing of dustbins ; but, for the most part, improvements
should be made only by degrees, as the people became more
capable of valuing and not abusing them. I would have the
rooms distempered and thoroughly cleansed as they became
vacant, and then they should be offered to the more cleanly of
the tenants. I would have such repairs as were not immediately needed used as a means of giving work to the men in
times of distress. I would draft the occupants of the underground kitchens into the upstair rooms, and would ultimately
convert the kitchens into bath-rooms and wash-houses. I
would have the landlady's portion of the house—*i.e.* the stairs
and passages—at once repaired and distempered ; and they
should be regularly scrubbed, and, as far as possible, made
models of cleanliness ; for I knew from former experience that

the example of this would, in time, silently spread itself to the rooms themselves, and that payment for this work would give me some hold over the elder girls. I would collect savings personally, not trust to their being taken to distant banks or saving clubs. And, finally, I knew that I should learn to feel these people as my friends, and so should instinctively feel the same respect for their privacy and their independence, and should treat them with the same courtesy that I should show towards any other personal friends. There would be no interference, no entering their rooms uninvited, no offer of money or the necessaries of life. But when occasion presented itself, I should give them any help I could, such as I might offer without insult to other friends—sympathy in their distresses; advice, help, and counsel in their difficulties; introductions that might be of use to them; means of education; visits to the country : a loan of books; a bunch of flowers brought on purpose; an invitation to any entertainment, in a room built at the back of my own house, which would be likely to give them pleasure. I am convinced that one of the evils of much that is done for the poor springs from the want of delicacy felt, and courtesy shown, towards them, and that we cannot beneficially help them in any spirit different to that in which we help those who are better off. The help may differ in amount, because their needs are greater. It should not differ in kind.

To sum up : my endeavours in ruling these people should be to maintain perfect strictness in our business relations, perfect respectfulness in our personal relations.

These principles of government and plans of action were not theoretical; they had not been *thought out* in the study, but had been *worked out* in the course of practical dealings with individual cases. And though I am able thus to formulate them, I want it understood that they are essentially living, that they are not mere dead rules, but principles, the application of which is varying from day to day. I can say, for example, "It is our plan to keep some repairs as employment for men out of work ;" but it needs the true instinct to apply this plan beneficially : the time to give the work, its kind, its amount, above all the mode of offering it, have to be felt out fresh on each fresh occasion, and the circumstances and characters vary so that each case is new.

The practical carrying out in any court of these various plans of action involved, as may readily be imagined, a great deal of personal supervision. Hence the "lot o' landladies" which excited the attention of the street boys. Several ladies, whether owners of houses or not, have worked there energetically with me since the property was bought; and when I use the word "we," I would have it understood to apply to these ladies and myself; it is often upon them that much of the detail of the work devolves.

But to proceed with the history of this court. Our first step on obtaining possession was to call on all the inhabitants to establish our claim to receive rents. We accepted or refused the people as tenants, made their acquaintance, and learnt all they might be disposed to tell us about themselves and their families. We came upon strange scenes sometimes. In one room a handsome, black, tangle-haired, ragged boy and girl, of about nine and ten, with wild dark eyes, were always to be found, sometimes squatting near the fire, watching a great black pot, sometimes amusing themselves with cutting paper into strips with scissors. It was difficult to extract a word; the money and dirty rent-book were generally pushed to us in silence. No grown person was ever to be seen. For months I never saw these children in the open air. Often they would lie in bed all day long; and I believe they were too ignorant and indolent to care to leave the house except at night, when the boy, as we afterwards found, would creep like a cat along the roofs of the outbuildings to steal lumps of coal from a neighbouring shed.

At one room we had to call again and again, always finding the door locked. At last, after weeks of vain effort, I found the woman who owned the room at home. She was sitting on the floor at tea with another woman, the tea being served on an inverted hamper. I sat down on an opposite hamper, which was the only other piece of furniture in the room, and told her I was sorry that I had never been able to make her acquaintance before. To which she replied, with rather a grand air and a merry twinkle in her eye, that she had been " unavoidably absent;" in other words, some weeks in prison—not a rare occurrence for her.

When we set about our repairs and alterations, there was much that was discouraging. The better class of people in the court were hopeless of any permanent improvement. When one of the tenants of the shops saw that we were sending workmen into the empty rooms, he said considerately, " I'll tell you what it is, Miss, it'll cost you a lot o' money to repair them places, and it's no good. The women's 'eads 'll be druv through the door panels again in no time, and the place is good enough for such cattle ás them there." But we were not to be deterred.

On the other hand, we were not to be hurried in our action by threats. These were not wanting. For no sooner did the tenants see the workmen about than they seemed to think that if they only clamoured enough, they would get their own rooms put to rights. Nothing had been done for years. Now, they thought, was their opportunity. More than one woman locked me in her room with her, the better to rave and storm. She would shake the rent in her pocket to tempt me with the sound of the money, and roar out "that never a farthing of it would she pay till her grate was set," or her floor was mended, as the case might be. Perfect silence would make her voice drop lower and lower, until at last she would stop, wondering that no violent answers were hurled back at her, and a pause would ensue. I felt that promises would be little believed in, and, besides, I wished to feel free to do as much, and only as much, as seemed best to me ; so that my plan was to trust to my deeds to speak for themselves, and inspire confidence as time went on. In such a pause, therefore, I once said to a handsome, gipsylike Irishwoman, " How long have you lived here ? " " More than four years," she replied, her voice swelling again at the remembrance of her wrongs ; " and always was a good tenant, and paid my way, and never a thing done ! And my grate," etc., etc., etc. " And how long have I had the houses ? " " Well, I suppose since Monday week," in a gruff but somewhat mollified tone. " Very well, Mrs. L—— , just think over quietly what has been done in the houses since then ; and if you like to leave, and think you can suit yourself better, I am glad you should make yourself comfortable. Meantime, of course, while you stay you pay rent. I will call for it this evening if it doesn't suit you to pay now. Good morning."

Almost immediately after the purchase of the houses, we had the accumulated refuse of years carted away, the pavement in the yards and front areas were repaired, dustbins cleared, the drains put in order, and water supplied. Such improvements as these are tolerably unspoilable, but for any of a more destructible nature it was better to wait. The importance of advancing slowly, and of gaining some hold over the people as a necessary accompaniment to any real improvement in their dwellings, was perpetually apparent. Their habits were so degraded that we had to work a change in these before they would make any proper use of the

improved surroundings we were prepared to give them.
We had locks torn off, windows broken, drains stopped, dustbins misused in every possible manner; even pipes broken,
and water-taps wrenched away. This was sometimes the result
of carelessness, and deeply-rooted habit of dirt and untidiness;
sometimes the damage was wilful. Our remedy was to watch
the right moment for furnishing these appliances, to persevere
in supplying them, and to get the people by degrees to work
with us for their preservation. I have learned to know that
people are ashamed to abuse a place they find cared for. They
will add dirt to dirt till a place is pestilential, but the more
they find done for it, the more they will respect it, till at last
order and cleanliness prevail. It is this feeling of theirs,
coupled with the fact that they do not like those whom they
have learned to love, and whose standard is higher than their
own, to see things which would grieve them, which has enabled
us to accomplish nearly every reform of outward things that
we have achieved; so that the surest way to have any place
kept clean is to go through it often yourself. First I go at
regular times, and then they clean to receive me, and have the
pleasure of preparing for me, and seeing my satisfaction; then
I go at unexpected times, to raise them to the power of having
it always clean.

Our plan of removing the inhabitants of the miserable
underground kitchens to rooms in the upper parts of the
houses did not, strange as it may seem, meet with any appro-
bation at first. They had been so long in the semi-darkness,
that they felt it an effort to move. One woman, in particular,
I remember, pleaded hard with me to let her stop, saying, "My
bits of things won't look *anything* if you bring them to the
light." By degrees, however, we effected the change.

I mentioned in my summary of our plan of operations, our
custom of using some of the necessary, yet not immediately
wanted repairs, as a means of affording work to the tenants in
slack times. I lay great stress upon this. Though the men
are not mechanics, there are many rough jobs of plastering,
distempering, glazing, or sweeping away and removing rubbish,
which they can do. When, therefore, a tenant is out of work,
instead of reducing his energy by any gifts of money, we simply,
whenever the funds at our disposal allow it, employ him in
restoring and purifying the houses. And what a difference five
shillings' worth of work in a bad week will make to a family!
The father, instead of idling listlessly at the corner of the
street, sets busily and happily to work, prepares the whitewash,

mends the plaster, distempers the room; the wife bethinks herself of having a turn-out of musty corners or drawers—untouched, maybe, for months—of cleaning her windows, perhaps even of putting up a clean blind; and thus a sense of decency, the hope of beginning afresh and doing better, comes like new life into the home.

The same cheering and encouraging sort of influence, though in a less degree, is exercised by our plan of having a little band of scrubbers.

We have each passage scrubbed twice a week by one of the elder girls. The sixpence thus earned is a stimulus, and they often take an extreme interest in the work itself. One little girl was so proud of her first cleaning that she stood two hours watching her passage lest the boys, whom she considered as the natural enemies of order and cleanliness, should spoil it before I came to see it. And one woman remarked to her neighbour how nice the stairs looked. "They haven't been cleaned," she added, "since ever I came into this house." She had been there six years! The effect of these clean passages frequently spreads to the rooms, as the dark line of demarcation between the cleaned passage and the still dirty room arouses the attention, and begins to trouble the minds of its inmates.

Gradually, then, these various modes of dealing with our little realm began to tell. Gradually the people began to trust us; and gradually the houses were improved. The sense of quiet power and sympathy soon made itself felt, and less and less was there any sign of rudeness or violence towards ourselves. Even before the first winter was over many a one would hurry to light us up the stairs, and instead of my having the rent-book and money thrust to me through the half-open door, and being kept from possible entrance by a firmly-planted foot, my reception would be, "Oh, can't you come in, Miss, and sit down for a bit?" Little by little the houses were renovated, the grates reset, the holes in the floors repaired, the cracking, dirty plaster replaced by a clean smooth surface, the heaps of rubbish removed, and we progressed towards order.

Amongst the many benefits which the possession of the houses enables us to confer on the people, perhaps one of the most important is our power of saving them from neighbours who would render their lives miserable. It is a most merciful thing to protect the poor from the pain of living in the next room to drunken, disorderly people. "I am dying," said an old woman to me the other day: "I wish you would put me where I can't hear S—— beating his wife. Her screams are awful. And B—— , too, he do come in so drunk. Let me go over the way to No. 30." Our success depends on duly arranging the inmates: not too many children in any one house, so as to overcrowd it; not too few, so as to overcrowd another; not two bad people side by side, or they drink together; not a terribly bad person beside a very respectable one.

Occasionally we come upon people whose lives are so good and sincere, that it is only by such services, and the sense of our friendship, we can help them at all; in all important things they do not need our teaching, while we may learn much from them. In one of the underground kitchens, I found an old woman who had been living there for twelve years. In spite of every obstacle, and in the midst of such surroundings as I have described, she was spotlessly clean, and had done the very best for the wretched place: the broken bars of the grate she had bound in their places with little bits of wire; the great rents in the wall, one of which went right through to the open air, she had stuffed with rags, the jagged ends of which she had actually taken the trouble to trim neatly with scissors; she had papered the walls, and as they were so damp that the paste was perpetually losing its hold, she patiently fastened up the long strips of paper fresh every week. With all this work for it, she had naturally become so fond of her little home that it nearly broke her heart to think of leaving it. So we determined not to tear her away from it. After a time, however, the force of our former arguments told upon her, and suddenly, one day, she volunteered to move. She has kept her new room, as one would expect, in a state of neatness and order that is quite perfect. She has since been growing less and less able to work, but she has always paid her rent, she has never asked for help, nor would she even accept the small boon of my lending her some money until she could give the due notice which would enable her to draw out her own savings from the bank where she had placed them. She has lived thirty-five years in London, a single woman depending entirely on herself, without parish allowance or other aid, and has had strength to keep up her standard of cleanliness and independence, and a spirit of patient trustfulness that is unfailing. Her life on earth is nearly over; she is now confined to her bed, for the most part quite alone, without even a bell to summon aid: yet there she lies in her snow-white bed as quietly as a little child settling itself to sleep, talking sometimes with a little pride of her long life's work, sometimes with tenderness of her old days in Ireland long ago, and saying gently that she does not wish to be better; she wants to go "home." Even in the extremity of her loneliness only a small mind could pity her. It is a life to watch with reverence and admiration.

We can rarely speak of the depths of the hearts we learn to know, or the lives we see in the course of our work. The people are our friends. But sometimes, when such as this old woman seem to have passed beyond us all, and to have entered into a quiet we cannot break, we may just glance at a life which, in its simplicity and faithfulness, might make the best of us ashamed.

Since we began our work in the court there has been a marked improvement in many of the people. I may just say, as examples, that the passionate Irish tenant, who locked me into her room, did not leave us, but has settled down happily, and has shown me more than one act of confidence and kindly feeling; that the old woman whose "bits o' things" would look nothing if brought upstairs, after having been long in a light room, has now asked for a larger one, having freed herself from a debt which cramped her resources, and has begun to save; and that the two dark-eyed children were ultimately won over to trust in us. Their mother—a most degraded woman —when she at last appeared, proved to be living a very disreputable life, and the only hope for the children was to get them away from her influence. My first triumph was in getting the girl to exert herself enough to become one of our scrubbers; and finally, a year ago, we were able to persuade her to go to a little industrial school in the country, where she has since been joined by a sister of hers, who turned up subsequently to my first visits. Unfortunately the mother absconded, taking the boy with her, while we were still hoping tò get him sent away to a training-school also; but, even in the short time that he remained with us, I had got some hold over him. By dint of making an agreement with him that I would myself fetch him at eight one morning, and help him to prepare his toilet so as to be fit for the nearest ragged school, I got him to begin learning; and when once the ice was broken, he went frequently of his own accord.

Opportunities for helping people at some important crisis of their lives not unfrequently present themselves. For nstance, soon after we came into possession of the court, I once or twice received rent from a young girl, whom I generally found sitting sadly in a nearly bare room, holding in her arms a little baby. She looked so young that I thought at first the baby must be her sister, but it turned out to be her own child. Her husband seemed a mere boy, and was, in fact, only nineteen. One day, when the rent was not forthcoming, I learnt their story. It appeared that an aunt had promised the lad a sovereign to set him up as a costermonger, if he married the girl; but he had not bargained for prepayment, and the promise was not fulfilled. This marriage-portion, which was to have procured them a stock of herrings, had never been forthcoming. This seemed an occasion upon which a small loan might be of the utmost use. I accordingly lent them the much-needed sovereign (which they have since punctually repaid), and thus saved the young couple from being driven to the workhouse, and gave them a small start in life.

To show further the various opportunities afforded us by our footing with the people, I will describe one of our weekly collections of savings.

On Saturday evenings, about eight o'clock, the tenants know that we are to be found in the "club-room" (one of the former shops of the court, and now used by us for a men's club, and for boys and girls' evening classes, as well as for this purpose of collecting savings), and that they may come to us there if they like, either for business or a friendly chat.

Picture a low, rather long room, one of my assistants and myself sitting in state, with pen and ink and bags for money, at a deal table under a flaring gas-jet; the door, which leads straight into the court, standing wide open. A bright red blind, drawn down over the broad window, prevents the passers-by from gazing in there, but round the open door there are gathered a set of wild, dirty faces looking in upon us. Such a semicircle they make, as the strong gas-light falls upon them! They are mostly children with dishevelled hair, and ragged, uncared-for clothes; but above them, now and then, one sees the haggard face of a woman hurrying to make her Saturday evening purchases, or the vacant stare of some half-drunken man. The grown-up people who stop to look in are usually strangers, for those who know us generally come in to us. "Well! they've give it this time, anyhow," one woman will exclaim, sitting down on a bench near us, so engrossed in the question of whether she obtains a parish allowance that she thinks "they" can mean no one but the Board of Guardians, and "it" nothing but the much-desired allowance. "Yes, I thought I'd come in and tell you," she

will go on; "I went up Tuesday——" And then will follow
the whole story.

"Well, and how do you find yourself, Miss?" a big Irish
labourer in a flannel jacket will say, entering afterwards; "I
just come in to say I shall be knocked off Monday; finished
a job across the park: and if so be there's any little thing in
whitewashing to do, why, I'll be glad to do it."

"Presently," we reply, nodding to a thin, slight woman at
the door. She has not spoken, but we know the meaning of
that beseeching look. She wants us to go up and get her
husband's rent from him before he goes out to spend more of
it in drink.

The eager, watchful eyes of one of our little scrubbers
next attract attention; there she stands, with her savings-
card in her hand, waiting till we enter the sixpences she has
earned from us during the week. "How much have I got?"
she says eyeing the written sixpences with delight, "because
mother says, please, I'm to draw out next Saturday; she's
going to buy me a pair of boots."

"Take two shillings on the card and four shillings rent,"
a proudly happy woman will say, as she lays down a piece of
bright gold, a rare sight this in the court, but her husband has
been in regular work for some little time.

"Please, Miss," says another woman, "will you see and
do something for Jane? She's that masterful since her father
died, I can't do nothing with her, and she'll do no good in
this court. Do see and get her a place somewheres away."

A man will enter now: "I'll leave you my rent to-night,
Miss, instead o' Monday, please; it'll be safer with you than
with me."

A pale woman comes next, in great sorrow. Her husband,
she tells us, has been arrested without cause. We believe
this to be true; the man has always paid his way honestly,
worked industriously, and lived decently. So my assistant
goes round to the police-station at once to bail him, while I
remain to collect the savings. "Did he seem grateful?" I say
to her on her return. "He took it very quietly," is her
answer; "he seemed to feel it quite natural that we should
help him."

Such are some of the scenes on our savings' evenings;
such some of the services we are called upon to render; such
the kind of footing we are on with our tenants. An evening
such as this assuredly shows that our footing has somewhat
changed since those spent in this court during the first winter.

My readers will not imagine that I mean to imply that
there are not still depths of evil remaining in this court. It
would be impossible for such a place as I described it as
being originally to be raised in two years to a satisfactory condition. But what I do contend is, that we have worked some
very real reforms, and seen some very real results. I feel
that it is in a very great degree a question of time, and
that, now that we have got hold of the hearts of the people,
the court is sure to improve steadily. It will pay as good
a percentage to its owners, and will benefit its tenants
as much as any of the other properties under my management have done. This court contains two out of eight
properties on which the same plans have been tried, and all of
them are increasingly prosperous. The first two were purchased
by Mr. Ruskin.

It appears to me then to be proved by practical experience,
that when we can induce the rich to undertake the duties of
landlord in poor neighbourhoods, and ensure a sufficient
amount of the wise, personal supervision of educated and
sympathetic people acting as their representatives, we achieve
results which are not attainable in any other way. It is true that
there are Dwellings' Improvement Societies, and the good
these societies do is incalculable ; I should be the last to
underrate it. But it is almost impossible that any society
could do much for such places as the court of which we have
spoken, because it is there not so much a question of dealing
with houses alone, as of dealing with houses in connection with
their influence on the character and habits of the people who
inhabit them. If any society had come there and put those
houses into a state of perfect repair at once, it would have
been of little use, because its work would have been undone
again by the bad habits and carelessness of the people. If
improvements were made on a large scale, and the people
remained untouched, all would soon return to its former condition. You cannot deal with the people and their houses
separately. The principle on which the whole work rests is,
that the inhabitants and their surroundings must be improved
together. It has never yet failed to succeed.

Finally, I would call upon those who may possess cottage
property in large towns, to consider the immense power they
thus hold in their hands, and the large influence for good they
may exercise by the wise use of that power. When they have
to delegate it to others, let them take care to whom they commit
it, and let them beware lest, through the widely prevailing

system of sub-letting, this power ultimately abide with those who have neither the will nor the knowledge which would enable them to use it beneficially;—with such as the London landladies described at the beginning of this paper. The management of details will seldom remain with the large owners, but they may choose at least trustworthy representatives, and retain at least as much control over their tenants, and as much interest in them, as is done by good landlords in the country.

And I would ask those who do *not* hold such property to consider whether they might not, by possessing themselves of some, confer lasting benefits on their poorer neighbours?

In these pages I have dwelt mainly on the way our management affects the people, as I have given elsewhere my experience as to financial matters and details of practical management. But I may here urge one thing on those about to undertake to deal with such property—the extreme importance of enforcing the punctual payment of rents. This principle is a vital one. Firstly, because it strikes one blow at the credit system, that curse of the poor ; secondly, because it prevents large losses from bad debts, and prevents the tenant from believing he will be suffered to remain, whatever his conduct may be, resting that belief on his knowledge of the large sum that would be lost were he turned out ; and, thirdly, because the mere fact that the man is kept up to his duty is a help to him, and increases his self-respect and hope of doing better.

I would also say to those who, in the carrying out of such an undertaking, are brought into immediate contact with the tenants, that its success will depend most of all on their giving sympathy to the tenants, and awakening confidence in them ; but it will depend also in a great degree on their power of bestowing concentrated attention on small details.

For the work is one of detail. Looking back over the years as they pass, one sees a progress that is *not* small ; but day after day the work is one of such small things, that if one did not look beyond and through them they would be trying —locks to be mended, notices to be served, the missing shillings of the week's rent to be called for three or four times, petty quarrels to be settled, small rebukes to be spoken, the same remonstrances to be made again and again.

But it is on these things and their faithful execution that the life of the whole matter depends, and by which steady progress is ensured. It is the small things of the world that colour the lives of those around, and it is on persistent efforts to reform these that progress depends; and we may rest assured that they who see with greater eyes than ours have a due estimate of the service, and that if we did but perceive the mighty principles underlying these tiny things we should rather feel awed that we are entrusted with them at all, than scornful and impatient that they are no larger. What are we that we should ask for more than that God should let us work for Him among the tangible things which He created to be fair, and the human spirits which He redeemed to be pure? From time to time He lifts a veil and shows us, even while we struggle with imperfections here below, that towards which we are working— shows us how, by governing and ordering the tangible things one by one, we may make of this earth a fair dwelling-place; and far better still, how by cherishing human beings He will let us help Him in His work of building up temples meet for Him to dwell in—faint images of that best temple of all, which He promised that He would raise up on the third day, though men might destroy it.

IV

THE WORK OF VOLUNTEERS IN THE ORGANISATION OF CHARITY.*

It is clear to those who are watching the work closely, and must even be apparent to those less conversant with the subject, that a great and growing conviction is abroad that our charitable efforts need concentrating, systematising, and uniting. There are many signs that this conviction is bearing practical fruit. All the thirty Poor-Law districts into which London is divided are now provided with committees for organising charitable relief. The formation of these committees has led gentlemen specially interested in the subject to come forward in various parts of London as candidates for the office of Guardians; several such candidates have been elected in St. George's, Kensington, Marylebone, and other parishes. Nor is the movement confined to London. Charity Organisation Societies, or others of a kindred nature, have been established in most of the large towns of England and Scotland. Conversation, newspapers, conferences, all bear witness how very generally it is now recognised that something ought to be done to improve our system of charitable relief, some co-operation secured between Poor-Law and charity, and some efficient means adopted to render alms less pauperising than they have hitherto been. It is becoming clear to the public that there is a right and a wrong, a wise and an unwise charity. Those who have the interests of the poor at heart are learning, more and more, to consult experienced people before taking any direct steps towards trying to help those who apply to them for aid; those who wish to give money are

*Macmillan's Magazine, October, 1872.

beginning to entrust it to enlightened committees, instead of endeavouring to distribute it themselves.

It becomes almost needless now to enlarge on the evils of " overlapping,"—that is, of various charitable agencies covering the same ground whilst ignorant of each other's proceedings ; or to dwell on the cruelty of the utter want of system which has hitherto prevailed—to point to poor families assisted by three or four agencies at times when they needed help least, and others neglected by all at times when they needed it most. It would not be difficult to give examples of these evils, and to show that they are inseparable from the condition of large towns wherever nothing is done to secure unity of action amongst those who are trying to assist the poor.

Much has been done. The evils of overlapping, on the one hand, and of neglect on the other, are being swept away wherever organisation committees, with their machinery for thorough investigation, and relief societies with their power to assist, are in existence. By means of this system of inquiry into the merits of cases a great degree of uniformity in dealing with them is secured ; no relief is given without due consideration, no poor person who chooses to apply can fail to have a hearing for his or her case, and similar needs will meet with a similar response. All this is no small gain. But now a new danger seems to be arising ; a danger lest, rushing from one extreme to another, we should leave to committees, with their systems of rules, the whole work of charity, and deprive this great organising movement of all aid from what I may call the personal element. The value of this element seems to me to be inestimable. Charity owes all its graciousness to the sense of its coming from a real friend. We want to bring the rich and poor, the educated and uneducated, more and more into direct communication. We want to enlist the thought, knowledge, sympathy, foresight, and gentleness of the educated in the service of the poor, and must beware of raising up barriers of committees between those who should meet face to face. There is beyond all doubt in almost every town a great amount of volunteer work to be had, which, were it organised and concentrated, would achieve infinitely more than its best efforts can now accomplish. There is always, however, a difficulty in calculating to any great extent on volunteer work, inasmuch as it is apt to be disconnected, desultory, and untrained.

It is true that where an energetic body of visitors is gathered together under able and vigilant guidance—where their districts are small, their visits frequent, their written records simple and complete, and gaps in their ranks quickly filled up, so that their work is not intermittent—they form a powerful agency for good.   Such societies are usually the first to see the importance of putting themselves into communication with other charitable bodies ; and when they do this, little improvement in the machinery is requisite.   But it is also sadly true that the work of a number of earnest and devoted volunteers is thrown away because their districts are too large, their duties indefinite, and their work unconnected with that of others labouring according to a definite plan.

Several things, then, appear to me to be evident :—(1) that if the poor are to be raised to a permanently better condition, they must be dealt with as individuals and by individuals ; (2) that for this hundreds of workers are necessary ; and (3) that this multitude of helpers is to be found amongst volunteers—whose aid, as we arrange things at present, is to a great extent lost.   The problem to be solved, therefore, is how to collect our volunteers into a harmonious whole—the action of each being free, yet systematised ; and how thus to administer relief through the united agency of corporate bodies and private individuals ; how, in fact, to secure all the personal intercourse and friendliness, all the real sympathy, all the graciousness of individual effort, without losing the advantage of having relief voted by a central committee, and according to definite principles.   The way in which this problem has been dealt with in one small district of London will be seen in the following pages.   Every district will, no doubt, have to deal with the question in a somewhat different way, which must be determined by its special circumstances ; but the subjoined sketch of a plan now in operation is given because it is always easier to see how a scheme will work when it comes before us as an actual fact, with a definite place and history, than when its bare principles only are laid down.

The working of the plan is not yet by any means perfect. There are many flaws still to be remedied, many breaks still to be filled up.   It might, perhaps, have been better to delay writing about it till the working was made more complete, had it not been that the plan has been successful so far, and that it promises to be increasingly so.   Besides, this seems the time when an account of a practical scheme for using individual work in conjunction with that of committees may be of real value.   The need of some such scheme is felt with regard to the Poor-Law.   The Poor-Law authorities have lately called the attention of Boards of Guardians to the success of the Elberfeld system, which depends on the careful and systematic inquiries of a large number of volunteer visitors. The Macclesfield Board of Guardians has already invited volunteers to aid it under the name of Assistant-Guardians. The same want is felt with regard to charity. On all sides we hear of people willing to give their time if only they could be sure of doing good. They are dissatisfied, they say, with district visiting, which creates so much discontent and poverty, and does so little lasting good ; they want to know of some way in which their efforts may fit in with more organised work.

In the district in which the following plan has been tried, the poorer inhabitants have for years been accustomed to make their applications for relief daily, between nine and ten o'clock, at a house situated in the centre of the parish. The mode of administering relief has been changed, but the house is still used for the reception of applications. The names are taken down, and one of the blank forms used by the Charity Organisation Society* is filled up with the account given by the applicant of himself and his circumstances. The form will then contain a statement of the names and ages, occupation, and earnings of every member of the applicant's family, his present and his previous address, the parish relief he receives (if any), the name of the club or benefit society to which he belongs (if there be such), the particular help he asks for, and the ground of the application. The form is immediately for warded to the Charity Organisation Society, who thoroughly investigate the information it contains by means of a paid officer. It is returned with its statements either verified or contradicted, and now shows, in addition to what it contained before, the report of the relieving officer, that of the minister of any denomination with which the applicant is connected, and his character as given by his previous landlord and other references. On the day when the application is first made, and the Charity Organisation Society apprised of it, a postcard or other message is sent to the visitor of the street or court where the applicant resides. This informs her of the application, and also that she is expected to send in on the ensuing Friday any information regarding the case which she may already have, or may learn from a visit paid during the

---

* N.B.—To save confusion, the District Committee of the Charity Organisation Society is throughout this paper spoken of as the Charity Organisation Society. This seemed the simplest way to distinguish it from the Relief Committee.

week. She at the same time gives her advice as to the best
way of dealing with the application. The Relief Committee
(of the constitution of which we will speak presently) meets
every Friday evening. They have before them not only the
valuable information of the Charity Organisation Society,
gathered, sifted, and examined by their paid officer and representative committee, but also the detailed account of a volunteer, who brings to bear on the case a fresher and more personal
sympathy than a paid agent ordinarily possesses, who has much
more patience to listen to, and probably more patience to
elicit the little facts on which so much may depend. Anyone
will appreciate the value of this who has had experience of
the difficulty of obtaining the evidence of uneducated people,
women more especially; they are nervously confused, they
cannot understand what are the real points of the case, nor
state them clearly; often the most important fact of all comes
out apparently quite by accident in the middle of a long
sentence after the terror of being questioned has worn off.
Thus the reports sent in, even by young or inexperienced
visitors, bring forward facts which might never have come to
the knowledge of the committee, while the reports of more
practised visitors are of still greater value, and not unfrequently
suggest far more efficient ways of helping poor families than
could have been otherwise devised.

The applicant himself comes before the committee. He
can thus explain his prospects, clear up any apparent dis-
crepancy of statement, talk over any new plan proposed by
visitor or committee, and receive, without delay, the answer to
his application.

Whatever grant is sanctioned, however, or whatever plan of
action is suggested, the visitor is entrusted with the management of it, so that where money is given it reaches those
helped through a kind friend ; and where some plan is recom-
mended, it is tried under the friendly and watchful eyes of one
who, owing to the advantages of education, should be wiser in
many ways than the applicant. Her power, at any rate, is of a
different kind, and may fill in his deficiencies.

The province of the Charity Organisation Society is that of
investigation only; while the province of the Relief Committee, before whom all the collected information is placed,
and before whom the applicant appears, is that of final decision
or relief. It dispenses the funds of the district, receiving
money from people of all denominations, and administering
help to all denominations without distinction. It is composed

of two clergymen, one doctor, one schoolmaster, three trades-
men. In order to secure the attendance of men occupied
during the day, this committee meets in the evening. One
lady, the referee of the Charity Organisation, always attends as
a medium of communication between the visitors, committee,
and Charity Organisation Society. Any visitors can attend
who wish, but in general they find it more convenient to report
by letter. Unless the referee has much time, one paid worker
is needed to carry out the work well. In the district just
described the former almoner is employed, who has great knowledge of the people. She attends the committee, and her information is found to be most valuable. It is a great advantage
to have someone always on the spot. She receives applications, and at once sends notice of them to the visitors and
Charity Organisation Society. She communicates to the
visitors the decision of the committee, pays them money which
is voted for applicants living in their districts, and keeps the
accounts. In cases of emergency she visits, but her main
object ought always to be to bring the visitors in well to their
work.

Such is an outline of the plan adopted as regards its main
features. Dry and formal as it may appear in print, I think
that anyone who reflects will see how the most intimate,
loving, friendly way of reaching the poor through the efforts of
kind visitors (each of whom visits chiefly amongst those she
knows best) has been secured, whilst any danger of confusion
has been avoided, and the chance of overlapping has been
reduced to a minimum.

A few specimens of the kind of cases which may come
before the Parish Committee, and of the mode in which they
would be dealt with, are here subjoined.

An old woman enters the room. She gives an anxious,
nervous glance at the members of the committee. who are
sitting round the table. She is asked to take a seat and to
answer the questions, which are as kindly put to her as possible.
Soon, however, she becomes hopelessly confused, and in her
long rambling tale contradicts herself over and over again. It
seems to be impossible to discover any reason for her actions
—why she lives in so dear a room, why she persistently hides
some facts. But reference is made to a note sent by the lady-
visitor to the committee. She, in a quiet, friendly talk, has
found out all the old woman's tale. The committee are thus
able to understand why she clings to the room she has lived in
for so long, though the rent is high ; why she works to keep a

lodger, when she might live as cheaply alone; why she refuses
to tell the names of those who help her. All is cleared up;
and since her relations seem to be doing their duty, and the
parish making the largest allowance which the Guardians think
it right to give outside the workhouse, a pension of two shillings
a week is granted her for three months. The visitor will pay
this pension, and in her weekly visit the friendship will grow.
She, unconsciously, perhaps, will supervise the home, and at
the end of three months, when the old woman will appear
again to have her pension renewed, she will be able to tell of a
life which has become quieter and happier.

Or perhaps a younger woman applies. She will tell how
illness and misfortune have reduced herself and her husband
to poverty. He has at length gone into the workhouse in-
firmary, where possibly he may linger on for months or years,
and she has come to ask for help for herself. The committee
see that the only result of a gift would be to destroy her power
of self-help, and to tempt her to lean on the uncertain aid of
others, while if they helped her adequately the tax on their
own funds would be large, and she would be kept in idleness
and prevented from fitting herself for future work. She pleads
for a little temporary employment, but they tell her that as she
has no children to need her care, she had better at once take a
place as domestic servant. She says she is not strong enough
for hard work. They elicit, however, that she is a good needle-
woman, and therefore advise her to seek a place as young
lady's-maid, or wardrobe-keeper in a school. Her reply is,
"Thank you, but I'd rather muddle on." The committee is
no doubt right; its decision will help her to face her future,
and to see that it is best now, while she is not old, to find an
occupation by which she can permanently support herself.
Yet she cannot see it at present in this light, it comes to her
too suddenly. In spite of the gentle considerateness of the
members of the committee, it must be hard for her to face her
fate, receive, as it were, the verdict, "No more home," from a
company of people she never saw before. The decision must
seem stern. But that night a letter will be despatched to the
lady who has charge of the district where she lives, telling her
the committee's decision; the visitor will gently talk to her,
advise her, perhaps find a situation for her; when she has
resolved to take one, the visitor will herself write to the
committee asking for a grant for an advertisement or for
clothes.

Others apply to whom the committee recommend a course

which seems hard. A little sick child must be sent away into the country. The father of a family must go to a Convalescent Hospital. The large and expensive room must be given up by the old couple whose wages are falling lower and lower. The kitchen, the dampness of which is sapping the children's strength, must be left; the idle son must be made to work. The advice of the committee is generally refused, but they need not despair. They know that in a day or two the visitor will call—she will tell the mother how kind are those who care for sick children, and will gradually persuade her to send her little one out of the hot, close air which is killing it. She will tell the man how much better it would be to get thoroughly strong than to work on in his weak state ; she will stir him up by thoughts of the bright grounds which surround the Convalescent Hospital; and soon she will come to the committee for the offered letter. Going day by day she will break down the apathy and carelessness which has allowed a high rent or an unhealthy situation so long to cripple the strength of the family. She will tell of better and cheaper rooms, she will appeal to both love and prudence, and by kind words to-day, and by stern refusals to-morrow, give help till they so far help themselves as to move. She will go to visit those who are bitterly resenting the decision of the committee not to help so long as the strong son remains idle, or children are kept away from school. She will speak gently and simply of the blessedness of duties; she will tell of the kindness which has seen so far that it would make the idle industrious, the careless careful, the ignorant wise. Perhaps she will find and talk to the truants, or the idler, and them she will induce to go with some of their playmates to school; him she will stir up to apply for the work of which the committee told him. Thus the visitor in her visits will persuade and rouse the people to the action that the committee saw to be good, but were powerless to enforce.

Then there are those who suffer poverty quietly and shrink from making any appeal. These the visitor finds out and sends to the committee for their advice and help. Spirited and hardworking women, high-class working men whose illness has been so long that the club money has ceased, will thus be brought to the notice of the committee, who will go patiently into each case. The woman will probably be offered some work ; and though she has a hard life at home, children to care for, and occasional mangling to do, she will make an effort to accept the offer; some means of cure or some quiet work will be pro-

posed to the sick man, or it may be thought well to grant him
a regular sum weekly for a time. In all the cases the knowledge of the committee will be brought to bear on the poverty
of the striving family that the visitor has discovered.

The visitor, however, may not always appear to advocate
assistance; sometimes she comes to discourage it. People
will apply whose tale seems good. A man wants work; a girl
wants clothes to go to a place. At first it appears as if they
would make good use of help. The visitor's report soon gives
another aspect to the case. She will tell how on such a date
the man had lost his work through drink, or how the help so
often received had been misused; it is clear to the committee
now that such a man can only learn by being left to himself,
and though he cringingly begs for work, it is refused. The
visitor will also tell how the girl has been frequently helped to
clothes of which she had made no good use; how situation
after situation had been carelessly lost, how weak parents and
idle companions had always been ready to back her up in bad
ways. The committee are thus able to see that now she must
be taught to earn her clothes gradually. So only will she
learn her responsibilities and reap the natural reward of
labour.

It will be seen from the foregoing illustrations that the
endeavour of the committee and of those at work under
them is to give help that shall be adequate, and, as far as
possible, permanently beneficial. They feel themselves bound,
even though the applicant be deserving, to refuse aid which
would be a mere temporary stop-gap and confer no lasting
benefit, and their aim is in every case to rouse the spirit of
independence and self-help.

It will also have been observed how very valuable an
element in the working of the scheme the visitor forms; that
she is not only a channel through which useful information
reaches the committee, but is, in almost every instance, their
actual agent in carrying out the plans of help adopted. I
must, however, say something further as to the importance of
the appointment of some lady or gentleman acting as *Referee;*
that is, as a centre for all the volunteers working as visitors.
For if volunteer work is to form a useful part of our scheme
of dealing with the people, we must accept those as workers
whose work is necessarily intermittent. This must be done
in order that we may secure a sufficient number of workers,
and not waste, but gather in and use all the overflowing
sympathy which is such a blessing to giver and receiver. With

our volunteers, home claims must and should come first ; and
it is precisely those whose claims are deepest, and whose family
life is the noblest, who have the most precious influence in
the homes of the poor. But if the work is to be valuable, we
must find some way to bind together broken scraps of time,
and thus give it continuity in spite of changes and breaks.
One great means of doing this is to have a living centre.
This should be secured in the referee.

The referee in the district here described was appointed in
the first instance by the District Committee of the Charity
Organisation Society ; she was subsequently asked to attend
the Relief Committee, and has since been recognised by the
Guardians and the Sub-committee of the School Board as the
representative of all the visitors throughout the district : the
Guardians kindly send to her, after their weekly meeting, notes
of every decision arrived at as to applications for relief; these
are immediately passed on by her to the visitor of the particular court where the applicant resides. The School Board
has withdrawn its paid agent, and entrusted to her and the
staff of visitors acting in concert with her the working of the
compulsory clauses of the Education Act. She thus acts as
a connecting link between all the various agencies at work in
the parish.

It is evident that a catastrophe would ensue if public
bodies, such as the Guardians or School Board, attempted to
deal directly with such a crude, changeful, and untrained body
as our volunteers necessarily form ; but, communicating with
them through the referee, they can use their aid and find it
valuable.

The existence of a referee is a help to the visitors in
various ways. She receives applications from all volunteers,
introduces them to the clergy and others who need workers,
or enrols them as visitors under the Charity Organisation
Society in unvisited courts, if such there be. She has nothing
to do with their work, so far as it is denominational, but takes
note of it so far as it deals with visible help. She introduces
temporary or permanent substitutes when visitors are absent
from town, or ill, or unable from any other cause to continue
their work ; so that the threads of it are never broken. She
is able to give, in a much more detailed and personal way
than any corporate body could do, information as to sources of
relief, societies available for special cases, as to what visitors
of other denominations are doing, and what help the Poor-
Law will give. For example: " Can anything be done about

Mrs. H——?" a new visitor will ask ; "her room is fearfully dirty, and she is so infirm now that she cannot keep it clean. She would be better off in the workhouse." "I will communicate with the Guardians, and no doubt the relieving officer will visit and report," the referee will answer. Or another volunteer will ask, "Can you tell me exactly what the law is now as to compulsory attendance at school? There are several bad cases of neglect in my court—what should I do about them?" Or another: "No. 7 in —— Street is in a most unhealthy state; can nothing be done?" "Yes, certainly," the referee will say; "if the drains are really, as you think, not trapped, the landlord can be compelled to do it. Write to the Inspector of Nuisances, and ask him to look into it. He is always most attentive to a request of this kind." Sometimes the suggestion will come from the referee. "Would you," she will say to some of the ladies, "make a list of the unvaccinated children in your streets, and tell the mothers how and when most easily to get the neglect remedied? They only want a little spurring up." Such is the work the ladies find, and the kind of help the referee can give.

Another most important means of securing unity of action is afforded by the written records which the committee make it a point that the visitors should keep—and should keep according to one fixed and definite plan. Each court has its own separate district book; each applicant has his separate page, where the detail regarding him and his family can be found at once. The reports of the relieving officer, of the clergyman, and of any references the applicant may have given, are all found in a condensed form on this same page. An entry is made of every kind of material help given, summed up in a money column each month; and the visitor is also expected to record every month the principal events which have happened in the family. One line only is allowed for this. This rule is made because MS. records become useless if they are voluminous ; the chief events only are required, and must be carefully selected. The book is sent in once a month to the referee.

The privacy of the poor is not infringed by the use of these records, since the books remain exclusively in the hands of the visitor and referee, and it rests with the visitor to report to the committee only that which she deems essential to the right decision of a case. And, moreover, nothing of a private nature—nothing which could imply a breach of confidence— ought ever to be entered in the books at all.

The advantages of thus keeping district books are very great. It is of course not unusual for those who visit amongst the poor to keep written records of one kind or another. But if they are kept in various forms, and the information is not tabulated so as to be readily comprehended by fellow-workers, half their value is lost. To be available for general use, it is all-important that the books throughout a parish should be *uniform*, and the information contained in them *complete* and *condensed*. They should be arranged so as to bring to a focus all the information obtained through the Charity Organisation Society. Now it too often happens that they contain only notes of such facts as have come under the visitor's personal observation, and are kept by each visitor according to a different plan.

The work itself is an always growing one, as the system does not stop at mere relief, but uses its machinery to carry out every plan of helpfulness that can be devised. The visitors find that the work opens out as they themselves increase in power. Then the question arises how the pressing, useful things, which so urgently need doing, can possibly be got through. "I see more to do in my district the longer I work there," one lady said to the referee, not long ago; "the more I learn, the more the work increases. I see numberless helpful things that I could do if only I had time. May I divide my district? I don't know which part of it I can make up my mind to give up; there are people I should grieve to lose sight of in every part of it, yet I cannot manage all that I now see ought to be done." "Do not divide your district," the referee replied; "the Committees, Guardians, and School Board, and I myself, cannot easily treat with still smaller divisions than that into separate courts or streets. Let me introduce you to one of the younger volunteers, whom you may associate with you in the work. She is too young to visit alone, or to judge what is wise in difficult cases, but she will write your monthly reports, will be a friendly messenger to pay pensions, will call to ask if children are at school and report to the School Board, will collect savings and keep accounts of them, will write about admissions to Convalescent Homes or Industrial Schools, will give notice of classes and entertainments, and register the window plants before our flower shows. In short, she will form a friendly link between you and the people, will save your time, and be herself trained to take the lead hereafter. Mr. R., too, offers help in the evening, if you want him to establish that Co-operative Store, to keep some life in the Working Men's Club, or to collect savings in the court on a Saturday night; and Mrs. S. offers help in money for special cases of want which the committee can hardly take up, or for some of our excursions to the country this summer. In fact, if you will associate other workers with you, instead of still further subdividing the district, it will be much the best."

And so the work grows, and the various help gets more and more woven into one whole.

Much has been written of late on the subject of Sisterhoods and of " Homes," where those who wish to devote themselves to the service of the poor can live together, consecrating their whole life to the work. I must here express my conviction that we want very much more the influence that emanates not from "a Home," but from "homes." One looks with reverence on the devotion of those who, leaving domestic life, are ready to sacrifice all in the cause of the poor, and give up time, health, and strength in the effort to diminish the great mass of sin and sorrow that is in the world. I have seen faces shining like St. Stephen's with sight of heaven beyond the pain and sin. I have seen shoulders bent as St. Christopher's might have been—better in angels' sight than upright ones. I have seen hair turned gray by sorrow shared with others. And before such one bends with reverence. But I am sure we ought to desire to have as workers joyful, strong, many-sided natures; and the poor, tenderly as they may cling to those who, as it were, cast in their lots amongst them, are better for the bright visits of those who are strong, happy, and sympathetic.

"Send me," said one day a poor woman, who did not even know the visitor's name, " the lady with the sweet smile and the bright golden hair."

The work amongst the poor is, in short, better done by those who do less of it, or rather, who gain strength and brightness in other ways. I hope for a return of the old fellowship between rich and poor; to a solemn sense of relationship; to quiet life side by side; to men and women coming out from bright, good, simple homes, to see, teach, and learn from the poor; returning to gather fresh strength from home warmth and love, and seeing in their own homes something of the spirit which should pervade all.

I believe that educated people would come forward if once they saw how they could be really useful, and without neglecting nearer claims. Let us reflect that hundreds of workers are wanted ; that if they are to preserve their vigour they must not be overworked ; and that each of us who might help, and holds back, not only leaves work undone, but injures, to a certain extent, the work of others.   Let each of us not attempt too much, but take some one little bit of work, and, doing it simply, thoroughly, and lovingly, wait patiently for the gradual spread of good, and leave to professional workers to deal for the present with the great mass of evil around.

To recapitulate, then, let me say that I think the operations of the Charity Organisation Society have been wholly bene-ficial so far, but that it will have to secure more extended personal influence between rich and poor if it is to be perma-nently successful.   As a society it is doing its work ; it is contending for justice and order ; it has urged us not to corrupt our fellow-citizens ; it has instituted inquiries in sup-port of truth ; it has responsible officers ; it is an upholder of method, and it will help us to be swift, just, and sure in our gifts.   But it can never be a more living educational body than the law is.   The society can never be a vital, loving, living force ; it can never wake up enthusiasm, nor gently lead wanderers, nor stir by unexpected mercy, nor strengthen by repeated words of guidance.   The ground once cleared by it, the work remains for individuals to carry on.

[N.B.—This article is reprinted, as the plan described in it appears equally desirable now, and worked well for some years.   It is not, however, in operation now.]

V

CO-OPERATION OF VOLUNTEERS AND
POOR-LAW OFFICIALS.*

SIR,—In accordance with your request, I beg to furnish an account of the system now in operation in a part of the parish of Marylebone, which aims at establishing a complete combination of official and volunteer agencies in dealing with Poor-Law cases.

The attention of Poor-Law reformers has been much directed of late years to the administration of outdoor relief in Elberfeld. The success of the system pursued there is no longer doubtful. It has been in operation for years : and the report presented to the Local Government Board by their inspector, after his visit, has proved how powerful it is in diminishing pauperism. In the first place, it is shown that the employment of numerous volunteer visitors has there formed a check on imposture, such as our relieving-officers, owing to the size of their districts, cannot possibly supply : and secondly, that it has been found possible to adopt there much more radical measures for removing poverty than are here adopted. The poor are divided into groups, each group consisting of a few families, and each cluster of families is committed to the special care and supervision of an intelligent visitor, who goes in and out among them, making himself acquainted with their daily lives, their past history, their present resources and circumstances.

This being so, an account of an organisation based on the same principles, and existing in our own country, gains an interest which it otherwise would not possess, and claims attention, though it covers a small area only, is only tentative,

* Report to Local Government Board, January, 1874.

and has not yet been in operation more than one year. If the
scheme succeeds and spreads, we may fairly hope much from
it. It is as yet in its infancy, and no formal opinion as to its
working has been pronounced by the Marylebone Board of
Guardians; but individual members of that Board have
expressed their warm approval; the clerk and the relieving-
officer appear much pleased with the plan; and at present
there are no signs of failure, nor does any modification even
appear necessary.

I proceed, therefore, to give an account of the system as at
present in operation, and will show afterwards its resemblance
to the Elberfeld plan, its chief difference from it, and the
reason why such marked difference is necessary here and
now.

At the end of 1872 it came under the notice of the
Guardians of St. Marylebone that there existed in a part of
their parish—the division known as St. Mary's, Bryanston
Square—a body of district visitors differing in some measure
from any to be found in other parts of London. Their special
training was due to the fact that soon after the Charity
Organisation Society was founded, the rector of St. Mary's
had determined to reform his system of distributing the funds
entrusted to him for charitable purposes, whilst still using the
district visitors as his agents. To this end he made over the
whole of these funds to a small committee, the St. Mary's
Relief Committee, composed of men of various classes, who
had given special attention to the wise administration of aid to
the poor. Every applicant for help throughout St. Mary's
had henceforth to appear before this committee, who were
guided in their decision as to his case both by a report from
the Marylebone branch of the Charity Organisation Society,
and by one from the visitor in whose district he resided.
Thus a thorough and efficient inquiry was secured. They
also aimed at making relief more adequate than formerly;
refusing small grants which would only give temporary and
illusory aid, and endeavouring, by means of employment,
emigration, loans to enable people to start afresh in life,
and so on, to give real and permanent assistance. This
committee I was asked to join, as, having a seat on the
Marylebone Charity Organisation Society, I could form a
personal link between the inquiring and the relieving bodies,
in addition to the written link which the report on each case
afforded. I was also asked to act as referee; that is, to
communicate the decisions of the committee to the visitor,

who was requested to dispense the aid voted or inform the
applicant of the reason of its refusal.   In this capacity of
referee, I formed a sort of centre for the district visitors; it
became my duty to give advice. when asked, and to instruct
new or inexperienced visitors in the nature of their duties and
the principles which they were expected to adopt.   Each
visitor had to keep a book, in which the name of every
applicant was entered, together with the information obtained
about him through the local branch of the Charity Organisation Society.   An account of all money given to him by any
charitable agency, and a short notice from month to month of
the events in his family were also entered.   Each book contained the facts relating to residents in one court or street
only, and was always in the hands of the visitor of that court,
temporary or permanent; an alphabetical index enabled her
to turn at once to the account of any given family.

The result of this system was to train a body of visitors in
judicious and organised modes of work.   The light thrown
upon cases of applicants by the Charity Organisation Society,
the advantages afforded by practical work under an experienced committee, and the power of watching individual
cases of distress through a long period of their history (a
power which small districts and written records materially
increase), were all important elements in the education of these
visitors.

When this system had been in operation two or three
years, it became clear that these volunteer visitors might be
valuable to the relieving officer, if they could be brought into
communication with him, and that a mass of information
had been collected in their district books, which might be of
service to the Guardians if it could be made available at the
right moment.   But the attempt to bring them into direct
communication with any official would have been open to
many objections.   Confusions might arise when visitors were
absent; new visitors would occasionally have to be appointed,
and to have their work explained to them.   No relieving
officer would have time to undertake this duty, nor even to
communicate with so large and fluctuating a body as that
formed by these volunteers.   The Guardians, therefore, resolved
to recognise one of these volunteers as representing the whole
body.   The referee would be a connecting link between themselves and the visitors, and through her only all communications would pass.   I was asked to fill this position with relation
to the Guardians, for one reason, because I was already a

member both of the Relief Committee before mentioned and the committee of the Charity Organisation Society, and the recognised medium of communication between these two bodies.

After the combination of volunteer and official agency had thus been arranged, which was in the winter of 1872–3, the Guardians directed the relieving officer who is in charge of the St. Mary's Poor-Law District, to send me daily a list containing the name of each applicant from that district, with his address, ages of family, and nature of application. I send out the information at once to the visitor in whose court the applicant resides, with a blank form, on which she may report any facts bearing on the character and circumstances of the family, which appear to her to be such as the Poor-Law authorities ought to know. She can report by giving a summary of the information contained in her district-book, and return the form at once, or she can revisit the applicant and give later information in addition if she deems it necessary. She sends her report to me, and I forward it to the relieving officer, who uses it as he may see fit. In many instances it gives information which the relieving officer might not otherwise possess ; as, for instance, that an applicant is in receipt of money paid by the visitor, or known by her to be paid by local charity. In other cases the report gives clues for further investigation by him, as where it mentions the existence of grown-up sons and daughters who may be able to give help.* After the weekly meeting of the Board, I am informed of the decision arrived at in each case, by a list sent to me similar to that furnished to every Guardian. These particulars I send to the visitors of the courts where applicants reside, and they are entered in the several district books. The average number of applicants in the Poor-Law District of St. Mary's is forty-five weekly, and the number of visitors engaged in the work is thirty-five. The number of visitors has doubled during the last year, so that we have subdivided all the larger courts and streets. Additional clergymen are coming into active co-operation with us, and some few gentlemen have come forward to act as visitors. These may all be considered hopeful signs that the movement is gaining ground.

* To prevent serious consequences in urgent cases, the relieving officer is authorised to give relief without awaiting the visitor's report. He is also bound to verify any statements which appear to require it. His responsibility to the Board is thus not weakened, while the information upon which he acts is more complete. Even when the information does not reach him until after temporary relief has been administered, it is still valuable for his future guidance.

It will be seen from this outline, that in St. Mary's district there are four agencies employed in the endeavour to administer relief to the necessitous in the wisest and most really helpful way : the Guardians, with their relieving officer, the Charity Organisation Society, the Relief Committee, and the District Visitors. These four agencies are connected and brought into efficient co-operation by the referee, who directs and superintends the visitors, attends the meetings of the Charity Organisation Society, and of the Relief Committee, and is the medium through which the Board of Guardians acquire information otherwise inaccessible to them.

The immediate direct effect of the adoption of this system upon the Poor-Law cases may be slight ; it may be that the information supplied by the district visitors does not in many instances modify the decision of the Board ; but this is the least part of the work. If the visitors really learn their duties, and apprehend the spirit of the system they have undertaken to carry out, it is impossible to measure the effect which their work may have in diminishing pauperism and inducing more provident habits of life among our labouring classes ; and thus, along with other advantages, reducing the heavy burden of the poor-rates. The connection with the Poor-Law system is calculated to be of great advantage to the visitors. They will learn something of its working ; they will be enabled to use with much greater effect, and with much greater frequency, the lever which distaste for the "house" puts into their hands ; and knowing that while the workhouse exists even the idle and improvident and reckless need not starve, they will be encouraged to refuse to such persons the pauperising doles of a merely impulsive charity, in the belief that such refusal will probably benefit the individual, and will certainly in the long run benefit the class.

The plan described resembles the one in operation at Elberfeld, inasmuch as it is based on the same principle ; subdivision of work among a large number of volunteer visitors, grouped under recognised, though unpaid, leaders. As at Elberfeld, we have not sought to enlist visitors who can give their whole time to the work. We want those living in their own homes, surrounded by their own interests and connections, and who can bring individual sympathy and thought to bear on a very few families. A large number of visitors is needed, and we could not obtain them if those only were eligible who could give a large amount of time to the work. Even more intimate knowledge of individual families is secured in Marylebone than we have any evidence of in the case of Elberfeld, because here in their own small districts the visitors undertake duties for other bodies as well as for the Guardians. Our volunteers are constantly in the courts, on business connected with the local charities, with the Charity Organisation Society, and also with the School Board; and though I must not here enlarge on the particular form of their work for these different bodies, I may point out that the entire truth is better elicited by those who come into communication with the poor in various ways : facts concealed from them in one capacity being revealed to them in another. For example, the desire on the part of parents to represent the ages of children to the Poor-Law visitor as young enough to receive parochial relief, is counteracted by their desire to represent them to the School Board visitor as old enough to exempt them from attendance at school.

The important difference between the Elberfeld and Marylebone systems is that, whereas in Elberfeld the volunteers themselves decide on the parochial relief, our volunteers have no such authority committed to them. It would be a fundamental change of the gravest nature to throw any share of such responsibility on the visitor, and would be a change not only disastrous, until the visitors have more experience, but in my opinion probably unadvisable even in the future. The large discretionary power exercised by Guardians under our English Poor-Law (which contrasts with the very definite scale for outdoor relief in use at Elberfeld) would make it an additional difficulty to place the decisions as to grants in the hands of visitors. In fact, in every case, so that only the evidence brought before him be sufficient, it is easier for a judge or arbitrator to deal in a uniform manner with cases which come before him when he is not brought into close communication with those whom his decision affects. So that the division of duty in Marylebone, where the visitor brings information and the Guardians vote relief, appears to be the right one. It is, moreover, a real help to the visitor in maintaining a satisfactory footing among the people under her charge, that they should know that, though she will listen to and represent their claims for relief, the absolute award of it does not rest with her.

I may perhaps here point out that there is one small addition to the system, which, though it would be of no direct advantage to the Poor-Law authorities, would be of great service to those who are administering the local charities. I have already mentioned that the Guardians send to me as

referee an official weekly report of the cases decided by them ;
but the grounds of their decision are not given, and often they
may be such as would, if known to us, influence grants from
the charities.   If the Guardians saw no objection to allowing
one or two representative volunteers to be present at their
weekly meetings, this information would reach us fully and
regularly.   It would also afford guidance to the visitors if we
could know to what extent the information furnished by them
to the relieving officer is received and acted upon.

There is one further addition to the scheme which has been
suggested.   It has been said that it might be well to empower
the volunteers to pay the regular outdoor relief of the aged at
their own homes, instead of compelling them, as at present, to
gather at the workhouse door to receive it.   As to the advantages
of this plan, I have as yet come to no decision.   On the one
hand, it is a gain that the poor should not be obliged to
congregate for relief, which has a pauperising effect upon them ;
and, moreover, the weekly visitation of the home would form
a regular method of inspection.   On the other hand, as I have
stated above, the less the visitor is contemplated as an almoner,
the more independent and satisfactory are her relations likely
to be with her people — and I fear the distinction between
bringing and giving relief would not be very clear to recipients.

In conclusion, I may say that the system described above
would, when perfectly carried out, insure that outdoor relief
should be confined to the deserving, and that drunken and idle
people should be offered the workhouse only.   Thus far our
volunteer workers are fully aware of the objects for which they
are associated together.   But I am myself satisfied that the
scheme is capable of a far deeper influence on the condition of
the poor, when the volunteers shall rise to the perception that,
in dealing with poverty, they must aim at prevention rather
than at cure ; at saving those under their influence from sinking
to the Poor-Law level, rather than merely obtaining relief for
them when they have reached that low point.   Few of my
fellow-workers have as yet grasped the idea that their best
success would be to develop the resources of the poor themselves, instead of letting them come upon the rates, or continue
upon them.   I think they rarely set before themselves the desire
to find some employment, at hand, or far off, which may support the young widow and her children before she has tasted
parish bread.   I think they rarely press upon the old woman
the duty of first trying if the successful son cannot support her,
or the daughters in service unite to do so.   They have not yet

watched the poor closely enough to see that this would be in reality the truest kindness. They forget the dignity of self-maintenance, they forget the blessing of drawing the bonds of relationship closer, and dwell only upon the fact that the applicant is deserving—see only the comfort or relief which the parish allowance would secure.

How far they can raise the people by degrees above the degrading need of charitable or Poor-Law relief, to be energetic, self-reliant, provident, and industrious, will depend upon the height of their own hope, the patience of their own labour, the moral courage which will teach them to prefer being helpful to being popular, and finally to the temper and spirit of their own homes and lives. For, say what we may, if our upper class were to become extravagant, improvident, and showy, it would be aped by those below it, even though as surely it would be despised. And if we desire to be the leaders of our poor into the ways of happy prosperity, we must order our homes in exactly the same spirit as theirs must be ordered—in simplicity, industry, and providence.

VI

WHY THE ARTISANS' DWELLINGS BILL
WAS WANTED.*

As some of the readers of this paper will know, it is now many years since I first began to interest myself in the condition of the houses in which the London poor are lodged, and the best means of making them cleaner and more wholesome than at present.

For a long time I hoped for success in this matter, chiefly from the gradual spread of individual interest and effort in the work, and the extension from street to street, and from court to court, of something like the system which I and my fellow-workers had inaugurated in the houses committed to our charge. But in the course of last year I for the first time began thoroughly to realise the enormous magnitude of the problem which must be dealt with, and the small progress which up to that time had been made in solving it. Moreover, it had become clear to me that there were obstacles to the successful prosecution of the work in certain courts and districts which neither societies nor individuals could, as things at present stand, hope to overcome. Perhaps a few examples of where the present machinery fails will illustrate my meaning better than general statements of principles.

I have lately been asked to take charge of some people and houses in a court in the neighbourhood of Drury Lane. For some years this court has been in the possession of a company, which has done its utmost in the way of expenditure to make the houses healthy and comfortable ; but the directors thought the tenants would gain something if I and my fellow-workers

* *Macmillan's Magazine*, June, 1874.

undertook the collection of rents, and thereby brought personal influence and care to bear upon the tenants. I went to the court to see what we could do further for the people and place. It is entered by a low archway under a house in a principal street, and has of course no roadway for carriages ; nor is there any exit at the end of it, a house which faces you as you enter the court blocking up the way. The court itself is ten feet wide. It contains houses of four, six, and eight rooms. These have each a little back-yard, in which are placed the dustbin and water-closet, and the cistern to supply drinking water. Exclusive of the ground covered by these, the yard is only three feet in length by four in breadth.

Immediately behind these small yards rise the back walls of houses which are in some cases much taller than the houses in the court, and make the back-yards like wells, into which the sun's light can rarely, if ever, penetrate. From these wells of yards the back rooms and staircases draw their only light, dim even at midday, when the sun shines brightly. I looked eagerly out for ways of increasing air and light, at least on staircases, which ought to be shafts of pure air to refresh the rooms so often kept shut up, so full of unclean stuffy furniture, bedding, and clothes, so full of people exhausting the air. But all that was possible had been done : there was a window on every landing, and though I at once saw that we could get the tenants to keep these clean instead of leaving black strings of dirt on every pane, and heaped accumulations of dirt on every ledge, yet most of the windows were wide open, so no cleanliness would increase the feeble gleam of light which was all that could descend between the high houses and surrounding walls ; nor could any draught of fresh air ever find entrance there. The houses all round belonged to owners who had no interest in awarding a larger share of light and air to the dwellers in the court. Nor was there any means of compelling them to do so, since no Building Act lays down the amount of distance which must be allowed between the walls of buildings which have stood where they do now for many years. All that private effort unaided by statutory power could do to minimise the evil had been or might be done. The intelligent and liberal owners of the court have done all they could to improve it. I, for my part, was ready to enlist the sympathy and educational influence of ladies who would train the people to cleanliness and order; but who among us could ever move back that great wall which over-shadowed the little houses, and made twilight at midday?

Who could give space to move the water further from the dustbins, and the drains further from the ground-floor windows? Who could remove the house at the entrance under which the archway passed, or that at the end, and let a free current of air sweep through the closed court? None of us. I was not surprised to hear that low fever was often there. I said to a woman, "You've a good deal of low fever down here." "Oh no," she replied, "not now; it *was* bad, but two died opposite last Tuesday, and two at the end on Saturday: we've not much now." "Not much!" I thought to myself as I walked sadly away.

Again, there was a court in Marylebone full of wild, quarrelsome, dirty Irish, a sort of sink into which the lowest people drifted when misfortune or wrongdoing were worst, and from which they rarely rose again. It belonged to a man who would not sell, and did not care to improve the condition of his people. At last, one day I happened to go down the court and saw, to my inexpressible joy, a great bill on one house, "To be sold by Auction." There was but one clear day to learn value, see lawyers and surveyors; but it was all done, and the lease of the house was bought by a gentleman who put it under our control.

A friend undertook the management of the house. Business takes her down there continually; she gets to know the people; she spends the money received for the rents, after all expenses and interest on capital have been paid, in improving the house. Water has been laid on; a new cistern placed instead of the defective and unhealthy water-butt. Those leading immoral lives are made either to reform or go. The elder girls are gathering round my friend, and beginning to feel her influence; she takes them flowers; she is training one or two for service. But she came to me one day with a grave face, and told me about the old woman who lives in the back parlour. She is very old, and has very bad rheumatism. No wonder, for the wall against which her bed stands—the only wall against which it can stand—is so damp that the water oozes out in large drops, not only at the bottom, but for three or four feet above the floor. I went down at once to examine and inquire. "All the houses are alike all down the court," said an old man. "It can't be helped. In my parlour I've put up match-boarding; it's ground-damp, and nothing can't be done." It was but too true. All the houses were alike, and it was ground-damp. But unwilling to adopt the match-board plan, which hides but does not cure the damp, I asked an architect to go and see whether, by underpinning the wall and putting in some non-porous substance, the damp might be prevented from rising. This, he agreed, was the only radical cure, but the underpinning would cost very nearly as much as the lease had. Moreover, what was worse, the house was old, and probably would not stand it. The only means of meeting the difficulty was to rebuild; and whatever we ourselves may resolve to do in this particular instance, in most such cases nothing effectual would be done. The cost of rebuilding would have to be borne by individual lease holders, whose term is often short, and who are frequently poor men; and sanitary inspectors naturally shrink from enforcing the law except in the most extreme instances. A house may be condemned and pulled down under Mr. Torrens's Act; but that Act gives no power of compensating the owner, nor does it empower any public body compulsorily to acquire the different interests in defective houses, though, in the absence of some such power, it is often practically impossible to satisfy all persons interested so as to get hold of the house and effect the desired reform.

Again, there are many houses which it would be most desirable in the interests of the class which inhabits them to buy and renovate; but which, on account of defects in, or even absence of title, no person or company intending to lay out money in improvements would ever venture to purchase. A man is found in possession who is willing to sell, but has no title-deeds. Such a person of course cares only to collect the rents and carefully abstains from spending anything on the property, for fear of losing the value of his improvements, should any one with a better title appear. I have met with many properties which I should have been glad to get under my care, but which difficulties of this nature have kept me from buying.

I was led more particularly to consider how these and similar obstacles could be overcome, and also to realise more clearly how little had hitherto been done by existing agencies, when I was acting as member of a committee called together last year by the Council of the Charity Organisation Society to consider the best means of improving the dwellings of the poor in London. Two facts which specially impressed me came out before that committee. All the societies, and all private persons whom the committee could hear of as having done any considerable work in building or adapting houses for the London poor, were asked to send in returns of the number

housed by them. Information was received from numerous
sources, including the Peabody Trustees, Sir Sydney Waterlow's Company, and the Baroness Burdett Coutts. It was
startling to find that, since the Metropolitan Association (which
was the first to begin the work) commenced its operations
some thirty years ago, it' and its successors had provided
accommodation for only 26,000 people—not a great deal more
than half the number which is yearly added to the population
of London !

And further, it came out that the difficulty in obtaining
satisfactory sites was such that Sir Sidney Waterlow's Company
had a large amount of capital in hand, which they could not
employ for want of suitable ground. And this while capitalists,
who care nothing and know nothing of their property, are
making money out of houses which are a curse to the neighbourhood !

But while we saw how much there was to do, and how
little comparatively had yet been done, and how hard it was to
devise adequate remedies, we were cheered by hearing that one
great city had already faced and overcome difficulties like our
own. We heard of an Act passed in the year 1866 for the
improvement of the city of Glasgow, and the Lord Provost
was kind enough to come and give us information as to the
nature and the working of that Act.*

He said that in Glasgow the population had long been
living huddled together in masses—50,000 people being
crowded into eighty acres. Many of the houses had been
without sufficient air or light, and many had been mere dens
of thieves and paupers. The promoters of the Act had come
to the conclusion that it was necessary to root out the evil, and
had applied to Parliament for power to borrow a million and a
quarter; had marked the bad parts on a plan, and had obtained powers to pull down, rebuild, or sell, as might be thought
best ; in fact, entirely to change the place. They had got
liberty to impose a rate of sixpence in the pound, but had only
found this necessary the first year; it had then been reduced
to fourpence for two years, then to threepence, and they were
now, he hoped, about to reduce it to twopence. They had
employed a surveyor quietly to buy up a large amount of
property before they did anything, as the prices would have
risen if they had begun to improve before completing their

* What follows is condensed from, a report of the Lord Provost's
speech, which appeared in the *Charity Organisation Reporter* of the 14th
May, 1873.

purchases. They had succeeded, with scarcely any disputes, in buying property to the amount of one million, and had resold, at a profit, upwards of £300,000 worth, selling the sites under restrictions for building. Fever houses had been removed, streets widened, and new thoroughfares run through the mass of buildings. Those to whom the working of the Act had been entrusted had not gone on the principle of building themselves; it had been sufficient to let the public know that houses were wanted—builders had rushed in and had built whole streets. Under their general Acts there was power to demolish only when a house was unsafe, not when it was in a bad sanitary condition; consequently, nothing could have been done without the powers of compulsory purchase and compensation given them by the Act of 1866. The trustees were restricted by the Act from removing more than 500 of the population at once, without a certificate from the sheriff that accommodation was obtainable; but, in fact, houses had been built to accommodate nearly double the number removed. The loss before commencing had been estimated at £200,000, but he did not now put it at more than £50,000, and even hoped to lose nothing by the work, though the expenses had been heavy—the cost of the Bill and Parliamentary notices to occupiers having been £17,000. The effect on the town generally was very beneficial. The houses of bad fame were reduced fifteen per cent., the haunts of thieves and of disease were broken up, the whisky shops had been reduced in number, and there was moral as well as physical improvement.

The importance of the precedent thus furnished was obvious and immense. The committee at once felt that here was the desired solution. If powers of compulsory purchase such as had been given to Glasgow, such as are given every day to railway companies, such as are conferred on the Metropolitan Board of Works, when streets are to be widened, or new thoroughfares made, could be vested in a body representing the ratepayers of all London, there would be some chance of effectually grappling with the evil in its entirety. Such a body might destroy houses, relet sites to builders or building companies, who would undertake to provide suitable dwellings; or should none such be forthcoming, might, in the last resort, itself undertake the task of rebuilding. It was suggested to the committee, that the absence of any municipal government for London, analogous to that of Glasgow and other large towns, would be a difficulty; but they were unwilling to postpone action until the very difficult task of organising a municipal government for London should be achieved; and they thought that the necessary powers might be entrusted to the Corporation in the City, and to the Metropolitan Board of Works in the remainder of London, for the present. Should the whole of London ever come to be governed by one central authority, the work and powers of the separate bodies might be handed over to the new governing power.

The committee drew up and published a Report embodying this view, and have since presented to the Home Secretary a memorial, expressive of their hope that the Government will take some action in the matter, and introduce a bill into Parliament containing provisions calculated to remedy the existing evils. But while I feel sure that the matter is in the hands of men who will not willingly let it drop, I feel also that at the present time it is important that every means should be taken to interest the public on the subject, and generate that force of opinion which makes realities of great projects. Feeling this, I hoped that a visit to Glasgow, and a report of what I found there, might do something to bring home to that large body of people, who find Blue Books and Reports unreadable, some notion of what has been done in Scotland, and might be done in our London.

I went, therefore, to Glasgow, and at once put myself into communication with the leaders of the movement there; and the first thing they showed me was the plan of the city as it was when the Act was passed, and photographs of some of the buildings which they had pulled down under its provisions. The unhealthiness and overcrowding must, I think, have been even worse there than in London. The "wynds," as they call them there, were at least as narrow as the London courts. Like them, they were often blocked up at one end, so as completely to stop the free passage of air. But I saw there—what I have seldom or never seen in London—a perfect honeycomb or maze of buildings, where, to reach the "wynd" furthest from the street, one had to pass under archway after archway built under the houses, and leading from one squalid court into another. Some of these narrow, tunnel-like passages appeared from the plans to have been many yards in length. The houses, too, were higher than is usual in London alleys, and the darkness and obscurity consequently greater. There was another feature completely new to me, and which certainly does not exist in London. Here and there, running up between house and house, were narrow crevices, from six to twelve inches wide, and from these the back rooms in some houses drew their only light. The existence of these crevices was explained to me in different ways. Some people said they represented spaces once occupied by garden walls, on which neither of the adjacent owners had a right to build; others, that the space was left that the eaves of each owner's house might drip on his own ground, and not on his neighbour's; and this latter explanation seems to be borne out by the common name of "dreepings" or "wastings" applied to these crannies. At any rate, there they are on the official plans, and I saw the remains of them on the spot—narrow spaces making houses better no doubt at first than if they had been built back to back, with no through draught. But when the habits of the people were dirty, and they threw things out of the windows, these dreepings, being far too narrow to be cleansed in any way, became receptacles where every kind of fever-breeding substance must gradually have decayed, carrying disease in every breath of air. As I looked over the official photographs of these "wynds," dark and dirty, and in every way degraded, and the chairman and secretary of the Trust which has had the working of the Act kept saying, "This is still standing—but *that* is gone," and "That is taken away, and that and that comes down next month," I could not help feeling how proud and glad these men must be to have achieved such reforms; and the longing rose strong in me that some one some day in London might be able thus to point to the sites of the old fever-dens, and say, "They are gone."

The next morning I went to see what remains of the old "wynds" and closes. I found that here and there a house, here and there whole sides of a close or alley, had been taken down to let in the brightening influence of sun and air. The haggard, wretched population, which usually huddles into dark out-of-the-way places, was swarming over the vacant ground for years unvisited by sun and wind. Children were playing in open spaces who had never, I should think, had space to play in before. I felt as if some bright and purifying angel had laid a mighty finger on the squalid and neglected spots. Those open spaces, those gleams of sunlight, those playing children, seemed earnests of better things to come—of better days in store. Of how bad things had been, of how bad they still were, I had curious proof. In some of the courts immense iron gates were standing, chained open when I saw them, but evidently capable, when closed, of entirely barring the thorough-fare. As they seemed to have been recently put up, I naturally asked why they were there. I was told that when houses were

removed which had previously blocked up one end of a "wynd,"
the thieves who haunt these places took advantage of the
passage thus opened to elude pursuit. To remedy this the
gates were put up : they are closed and locked at dusk, but the
police have a master-key, so that they can pass through to
pursue, while the fugitives are hampered in their efforts to
escape. Merely to break in upon these nests of thieves cannot but be a great good. Some kinds of wrong are not
decreased by scattering them, but dishonesty thrives most when
fostered in such dens. The near presence of honest, respectable neighbours makes habitual thieving impossible ; just
as dirty people are shamed into cleanliness when scattered
among orderly, decent folk, and brought into the presence of
the light.

I found that the new dwellings for the poor, which the
demolition of their old quarters had rendered necessary, had
for the most part been built, not on the old sites but in the
suburbs, upon land bought for that purpose by the trustees of
the Act, and by them leased to builders, who were bound to
erect workmen's tenements. These new dwellings were of a
type superior to those previously inhabited by artisans in the
city, and they have accordingly largely resorted there, leaving
their old abodes to be occupied by those displaced from the
demolished "wynds" and courts. It is of course far better
that the new houses should be thus erected by people who
take up the work as a commercial enterprise than by any
municipal body or benevolent society ; and the framers of the
Act had hoped that this would be done. But to secure the
Act from failing of its object, powers were conferred on the
trustees, which enabled them to undertake the work of reconstruction should they find it necessary. But it was not necessary : speculators readily came forward, and building of new
dwellings by private enterprise more than kept pace with the
removal of the old houses. This prompt supply of substituted
houses must have tended to prevent the rise in prices which
might otherwise have occurred had the displaced population
been left—as they have too often been left in London when
large blocks of houses have been removed—to compete for
lodgings in neighbourhoods already overcrowded.

Moreover, in Glasgow special care has been taken to
enforce laws against overcrowding; and, as already mentioned,
the special Act most wisely provides that not more than 500
people shall be removed in six months, unless the sheriff issue
a certificate that he has been satisfied that enough houses are

standing empty to lodge the displaced population. This pro-
vision, I was assured, had been rigidly complied with.

Glasgow, then, has not only got an Improvement Act, but
has carried it into effect in such a way as to bring about the
entire sanitary reform of the city. Now, are there any difficulties which should hinder London from achieving a like success?
There is but one point of difference likely, as it appears to me,
vitally to affect the question, and that is the great distance of
our suburbs from some of our most crowded districts. In
Glasgow, as I have said, cheap land could be had in the out-
skirts, and within a mile of the "wynds" which had to be
destroyed. The workmen who went to live there are not too
far from their work, and are easily and cheaply transported to
and fro by the numerous tramway cars which run into the very
heart of the city. But our suburbs are too far away for us to
hope that the majority of our poor, or even of our skilled workmen, can live there. Many might go—perhaps we hardly
realise how many. For these, of course, workmen's trains and
tramways should be encouraged; and will, no doubt, be provided as the suburban population increases. Extension of the
number of compulsory workmen's trains, and enforcement of
an earlier hour for their arrival at the terminus, might be
advisable. We may also hope something from the decentral-
isation of industry, and the likelihood of factories following
workmen to the suburbs if it become easier to get hands
there. But when all this is granted to the full, there would
remain, at least for many years, a certain number—I believe a
very large number—who must live near their work, and whose
work must be in London. How are the wants of these to be
met? The difficulty is the greater because they are likely to
be the poorest. Those who earn high wages can afford to pay
for trains and trams; they have shorter and more fixed hours
for work, and do not need to engulf all their families in the
vortex of labour, but can leave their wives and children in
suburban houses. But the widowed charwoman, obliged to
run home and get the children's dinner, the dock-labourer, the
costermonger, how shall their needs be met? For these and
many others cheap dwellings would have to be provided in the
neighbourhood of their present homes.

The problem is, how to do this without either raising the
rents to a prohibitory height, or committing the fatal mistake
of attempting to house a large population by charity. Now
numerous experiences have convinced me that houses may be
bought, pulled down, and rebuilt, and the rooms in the new

buildings let at less than the rent which was paid in the original houses, and yet a return of £5 per cent. net profit be made to the landlord on all moneys laid out, whether in purchase, demolition, or building operations.* This result has been repeatedly achieved under conditions in many respects less favourable than those which would often be present when people were working on a large scale, and with greater areas to deal with. For instance, where the houses were of two storeys only, the height could be raised, and the accommodation, and consequently the rental increased, whilst in covering large spaces with buildings constructed on a regular and systematic plan, much space would be gained which is at present wasted, owing to the fact that streets have been built and houses run up in a haphazard way, and at different times. How strikingly this sometimes is the case will appear from a statement of the Metropolitan Dwellings Association, that "while the population of Westminster (the most densely populated part of the metropolis) is only 235 persons to an acre, they can house 1,000 persons to the acre, including in the area the large courtyards and gardens attached to their blocks."†

But supposing that to pull down and rebuild houses on an improved. plan is not so expensive and wasteful as might at first sight be supposed, would it not be unwise to put half London into the hands of public authorities, and make them responsible for the building, management, supervision, and leasing of hundreds of thousands of houses? The answer is easy! Though it might be prudent to put into the Improvement Act clauses which would empower the municipal authorities to rebuild should no other agency come forward, yet the experience of Glasgow, as well as the probabilities of the matter, suggest that other agencies would come forward, and that private enterprise would be sure to do all that was wanted. As soon as the ground was cleared—perhaps even before it was cleared—companies and private builders would see their way to a profitable undertaking, and, as at Glasgow

---

* I give my latest experience of this kind here. Some houses lately purchased in a crowded court, the rooms of which were let at an average rental of 3s. 0½d., have just been rebuilt, and are let at an average rent of 2s. 7½d. a room, though many conveniences have been provided which were lacking in the old habitations, and there are no longer any rooms underground. The rents in many of the improved buildings seem higher in proportion than they are, because people compare a *set* of new rooms with a single old room.

† Quoted, with confirmatory evidence, in the Report of the Dwellings Committee of the Charity Organisation Society, p. 11. Longmans.

(where, by-the-way, there are no philanthropic building societies), would soon come in and replace the condemned dwellings by buildings of the kind required.

And now I have little more to say, except to make one or two suggestions which may perhaps throw some light on the problem of reconstruction, and the way in which it must be worked out.

One great element of cost in building a London house is the expense of the site. In some parts of the town each square inch has its price. To use the space acquired to the best advantage, and with the strictest economy compatible with due regard to sanitary requirements, must be the first object of the builder ; and in considering how to secure this end, we must remember that frontage to a thoroughfare is a great element in determining price. The sites, therefore, which abut upon the busier streets must not be used for the dwellings of the poor, if their rents are to be kept sufficiently low ; and yet the poor often require to be lodged in the im- mediate neighbourhood of these streets. We have also to remember that in most cases the houses in the main thorough- fares would not have to be disturbed, and that consequently the lines of London, as it stands at present, would be to a great extent left unchanged.

But we perpetually find in crowded parts of London blocks of houses built after this fashion : we have, first of all, a square of larger houses facing four streets. These once had gardens, yards, or spaces at the back ; but as land became more valuable these have been built over, usually with much lower houses, to which access is gained by a narrow passage from one or more of the thoroughfares, sometimes open to the sky, sometimes a mere tunnel under the house. It is these inner and lower houses which usually form the alleys and courts, and would be the proper subjects of demolition ; but the space gained by their destruction could not be effectively used unless power were given to break through the inclosing line of overshadowing houses, and make a way for the free passage of air. For this purpose power would have to be taken, not only over the houses whose state and position rendered their removal imperative or advisable, but also over so many of the more substantial houses as would need to be pulled down for the benefit of their humbler neighbours. Then, supposing our square space cleared and its approaches unroofed and widened, we shall use it to the best advantage by substituting for several courts of low houses (without well-planned relations to one another or to the houses in main thoroughfares) a single line or block of central dwellings. These must be much higher than the buildings they replace, so as to accommodate the same number of people, while leaving ample space between the inner block and the encircling shops and dwellings which face the streets.

But it is still probable, when all is done, that the poor may have to pay a little more for the substituted houses than they pay for their present dwellings, if sanitary reformers and philanthropic enthusiasts insist on elaborate appliances, costly to erect, and costly also to keep in order. To these latter I say, Do not aim too high. Be thankful to make any reasonable progress. It is far better to prove that you can provide a tolerable tenement which will pay, than a perfect one which will not. The one plan will be adopted, and will lead to great results ; the other will remain an isolated and unfruitful experiment, a warning to all who cannot or will not lose money. If you mean to provide for the family that has lived hitherto in one foul dark room, with rotten boards saturated with dirt, with vermin in the walls, damp plaster, smoky chimney, approached by a dark and dangerous staircase, in a house with no through ventilation or back-yard, with old brick drains, and broken-down water-butt without a lid ; be thankful if you can secure for the same rent even one room in a new, clean, pure house. Do not insist on a supply of water on every floor, or a separate wash-house for each family, with its greatly-increased expense of water-pipes and drainage. Build a large laundry which shall be common to the whole house, and in other ways moderate your desires somewhat to suit the income of your tenant. Give him by all means as much as you can for his money, but do not house him by charity, or you will house few but him, and discourage instead of stimulating others to build for the poor.

VII

SPACE FOR THE PEOPLE.

THERE is perhaps no need of the poor of London which more prominently forces itself on the notice of anyone working among them than that of space.

When I am in their rooms, I feel often how much even a foot or two would be worth, if the room were only large enough to let the wife open the window without climbing on the bed, or if she could get further away from the hot fire on a June day, or if everyone who came in wasn't forced to brush against the wall so that a great black mark quickly showed itself on the newly distempered surface.

I go into the back-yards, and how I long to pull down the flat blank wall darkening the small rooms, or to push it back and leave a little space for drying clothes, for a small wash-house, for the barrow to stand; and when I look at the unused bits of ground around a farm or cottage, I sometimes think what they would be worth at the back of a London house.

But even in the front of their houses in a London court are the poor much better off? I go sometimes on a hot summer evening into a narrow paved court, with houses on each side. The sun has heated them all day, till it has driven nearly every inmate out of doors. Those who are not at the public-house are standing or sitting on their door-steps, quarrelsome, hot, dirty; the children are crawling or sitting on the hard hot stones till every corner of the place looks alive, and it seems as if I must step on them, do what I would, if I am to walk up the court at all. Everyone looks in everyone else's way, the place echoes with words not of the gentlest.

In fact it is on such evenings that the drinking is wildest, the fighting fiercest, and the language most violent. A friend of mine at the East of London once said to me, " The winter does not try us half as much as the summer ; in the summer the people drink more, live more in public, and there is more vice." Sometimes on such a hot summer evening in such a court when I am trying to calm excited women shouting their execrable language at one another, I have looked up suddenly and seen one of those bright gleams of light the summer sun sends out just before he sets, catching the top of a red chimney-pot, and beautiful there, though too directly above their heads for the crowd below to notice it much. But to me it brings sad thought of the fair and quiet places far away, where it is falling softly on tree, and hill, and cloud, and I feel as if that quiet, that beauty, that space, would be more powerful to calm the wild excess about me than all my frantic striving with it—Lowell's words come into my mind,

> God's *passionless* reformers—
> Influences that purify, and heal, and are not seen.

The words reproach my own passionate efforts at reform, and set me asking myself whether we cannot find remedies more thorough, and supply in some measure the healing gift of space.

It is strange to think it must be a gift recovered for Londoners with such difficulty. To most men it is an inheritance to which they are born, and which they accept straight from God as they do the earth they tread on, and light and air, its companion gifts. In one way this fact makes the problem easier to deal with. This space it seems is a common gift to man, a thing he is not specially bound to provide for himself and his family ; where it is not easily inherited it seems to me it may be given by the state, the city, the millionaire, without danger of destroying the individual's power and habit of energetic self-help. The house is an individual possession, and should be worked for, but the park or the common which a man shares with his neighbours, which descends as a common inheritance from generation to generation, surely this may be given without pauperising.

How can it best be given ? And what is it precisely which should be given ? I think we want four things. Places to sit in, places to play in, places to stroll in, and places to spend a day in. As to the last named, I will not dwell on it here. The preservation of Wimbledon and Epping shows that the need is increasingly recognised. But a visit to Wimbledon, Epping, or Windsor means for the workman not only the cost of the journey but the loss of a whole day's wages; we want, besides, places where the long summer evenings or the Saturday afternoon may be enjoyed without effort or expense.

First, then, as to places to sit in. These should be very near the homes of the poor, and might be really very small, so that they were pretty and bright, but they ought to be well distributed and abundant. The most easily available places would be our disused churchyards. I have myself no fear that the holy dead, or those who loved them, would mind the living sharing in some small degree their quiet. There is a small, square, green churchyard in Drury Lane, and even the sight of its fresh bright verdure through the railings is a blessing; but if the gates could be opened on a hot summer evening, and seats placed there for the people, I am sure the dwellers about Drury Lane would be all the better for it. Again, round St. Giles's Church there is space for many seats under the trees. The number of people to be seen in Leicester Square (since the garden was thrown open to the public) show how glad people are of a seat in the open air. But Leicester Square shows us also another thing: such places must be made bright, pretty, and neat—a *small* place which is not so becomes painfully dreary, and it is quite curious to notice how little one feels shut in when the barriers are lovely, or contain beautiful things which the eye can rest on. The small inclosed leads which too often bound the view of a back dining-room in London oppress one like the walls of a prison; but a tiny cloistered court of the same size will give a sense of repose; and colour introduced into such inclosed spaces will give them such beauty as shall prevent one from fretting against the boundaries. Strange and beautiful instance this of how—if we recognise the limitations appointed for us, accept them, and deal well with what is given—the passionate longing for more is taken away and a great peace hallows all. Let, then, our small open spaces look well cared for. If they are not large enough to be opened to the public without limit, open them under restrictions, lend the key to district visitors, to the schoolmistress, to the clergyman, to the biblewoman, let them take in small companies of the poorest by turns. But make the most of what small spaces you have; do not close them wholly because you cannot open them wholly.

Secondly, the children want playgrounds. I am glad the Board Schools are providing these, and I wish they would arrange to have them rendered available after school hours, and on the Saturday holiday. So far as I know, this is not done. If it were, children would not be obliged to play in alleys and in the street, learning their lessons of evil, in great danger of accident, and without proper space or appliances for games. Such playgrounds, however, must be supervised. Mr. Ruskin provided one nine years ago in one of the courts of which I have charge, and we found then, and have found since, that it was necessary to have someone to keep order, and that it was a great gain to have ladies who would teach the children to play at games ; but the whole subject is so admirably explained in the *Sanitary Record* for July 25th, 1874, that I need do no more than refer to it here; but it may be useful to add tha supervision need not be costly. If a man of respectable character, too old to compete with younger workmen, were employed to take care of such a playground, it would be a double charity, such as many a kind donor might be willing to grant.

And, thirdly, we come to the places to stroll in. We could not have a better instance than the Embankment. What a boon it has been to London! Of course the parks come under this head ; and to what thousands of people they give pleasure ! But beyond these thousands are many who never find their way to these open spaces. Many notice the numbers who go to them ; a few of us know the numbers who do *not* go. Brought up in dirt, close quarters, and the excitement of the street tragedies ; ashamed of their neglected clothes; shy of a neatly-dressed public, they burrow in courts and alleys out of sight, when they might avail themselves of Park and Embankment. What the Ladies' Sanitary Association did by their park parties for the children, ought to be done for them also. They must be invited to come out in little companies for a walk, taken out again, and again, and again during the summer. In one of the worst courts under my care we have a small institute for the women and elder girls, where they have classes, and a common sitting-room, and entertainments in winter ; but I do believe one of the best things the Institute has done has been to arrange expeditions every Saturday during the summer, to park, or field, or common. The members pay all expenses themselves, and therefore they want places which they can reach by walking, or for a *very* cheap fare. I only refer to this as a specimen of the kind of thing that will become more and more frequent because it meets a great want —that of happy outdoor amusement, within short distance of

their homes, for those who have no gardens, no back-yards—
rarely a second room.

There are a few fields just north of this parish of Marylebone which indeed first put it into my head to write this article,
though the thoughts contained in it have long been before me.
These fields have been our constant resort for years : they are
within an easy walk for most of us, and a twopenny train takes
the less vigorous within a few yards of the little white gate by
which they are entered. They are the nearest fields on our
side of London ; and there on a summer Sunday or Saturday
evening you might see hundreds of working people, who have
walked up there from the populous and very poor neighbourhood of Lisson Grove and Portland Town. Fathers, with a
little girl by each hand, the mother with the baby, sturdy little
boys and merry little girls—as they entered the small, white
gate, you might see them spread over the green open space
like a stream that has just escaped from between rocks.
They sit down on the grass ; the baby grabs at the daisies, the
tiny children toddle about, or tumble on the soft grass, the
mother's arms are rested, and there she sits till it is time to
return ; or perhaps they go on up to Hampstead Heath, to
which these fields lead, which many could not reach, if these
acres were covered with villas, instead of affording a welcome
rest. Acres of villas! Yes, at last, the fields will be built
over, if they cannot be saved. They are now like a green
hilly peninsula or headland, stretching out into the sea of
houses ; the nearest fields I know to London anywhere ;
certainly the nearest on our side. The houses have crept
round their feet, and left them till now for us. I knew them
many years ago, when I used to walk out of London alone ;
and since then I have been there, as I say, with dozens
of parties of the poor. There the May still grows ; there
thousands of buttercups crown the slope with gold :
there, best of all, as you ascend, the hill lifts you out of
London, and will always lift you out of it, even when
houses are built all round ; for far away the view stretches
over blue distances to the ridge where Windsor stands. As
you come home—yes, as your children's children come home
—if you will save the fields from being built over now, will be
seen from them the great sun going down, with all his clouds
about him, or the fair space of cloudless summer sky, London
lying hushed below you—even London hushed for you for a
few minutes, so far it lies beneath—though you will be in it in
a short ten minutes.

These fields may be bought now, or they may be built over : which is it to be? The owner has given those who would like to keep the fields open time to see if they can raise the money to purchase them for the people for ever. He offers liberal terms, but they will still cost a great deal. Necessarily, fields near London *must* cost much. The question is, are they worth buying? To my mind they are even now worth very much ; but they will be more and more valuable every year—valuable in the deepest sense of the word ; health-giving, joy-inspiring, peace-bringing. But they will not be bought without considerable effort. Hampstead, which is on their north, cares comparatively little for them, having the heath on the further countryward side, though such fields between her and London must be a gain. No doubt Hampstead will do something ; St. John's Wood will probably do more, because these fields are to her, as to us, the nearest country walk. Marylebone ought, I think, to help a great deal, if she realises what a blessing those fields are ; but I doubt if all three districts can or should do all. I feel myself as if the question ought, in a measure, to be taken up by the large London landowners. They can, even when they try most, give their tenants so small a portion of space—the value of land in any central position being so enormous—that if they were asked for a few yards they would pause ; if for large open spaces, they would say, " It is impossible." The squares they have let to the rich, who will not now in some cases even lend them one Saturday afternoon at the end of the season to the poor of their own district for a flower-show, though if the grass were trampled quite brown, which is the only harm that could be done, another week would find the rich residents in the country among almost measureless green fields and glades. Some of these evils are perhaps unavoidable, but the possession of the land is a very great responsibility, and if there be so *very* little land on their own estates which they can dedicate to the service of the poor, surely they might feel it incumbent on them to do the next best thing, that is, to secure and throw open such fields as lie nearest to London on any side. The same duty appears to me to lie before the Corporation and the City Companies, and the more because the poor, having been a good deal driven out, the funds left for their benefit from the City, which these bodies have inherited, might well be applied to such an object as this. The Metropolitan Board of Works has, I understand, done a good deal in keeping and buying open spaces, but yet more is needed, I believe, and perhaps they may see their way to help.

It is a bad thing trying to see other people's duties: they alone can judge what they are. I can only hope that various people will take the question into consideration. I don't know absolutely that the fields of which I have written are the cheapest to be had, nor that there may not be others nearer to dense centres of population. I happen to know the special beauties of these, and their value to our side of London, and to be personally very fond of them, which somewhat disqualifies me from judging of their *relative* value. I would not, therefore, plead for *these* fields in contradistinction to others, though they have their special beauty. What I wish to urge—and I have only introduced a practical example now vividly in my own mind as most strongly bringing home the fact—is, the immense value to the education and reformation of our poorest people of some space near their homes, or within reasonable distance of them. We all need space; unless we have it we cannot reach that sense of quiet in which whispers of better things come to us gently. Our lives in London are over-crowded, over-excited, over-strained. This is true of all classes; we all want quiet; we all want beauty for the refreshment of our souls. Sometimes we think of it as a luxury, but when God made the world, He made it very beautiful, and meant that we should live amongst its beauties, and that they should speak peace to us in our daily lives.

THE BITTER CRY

OF

OUTCAST LONDON

AN INQUIRY INTO

THE CONDITION OF

THE ABJECT POOR

ANDREW MEARNS

LONDON, 1883

. We desire thankfully to acknowledge the assistance kindly afforded us in the pursuit of our investigations by the Secretary and Agents of the London City Mission, and also by the Rev. A. G. BROWN of the East London Tabernacle, and his Missionaries.

All communications should be addressed to Rev. ANDREW MEARNS, London Congregational Union, Memorial Hall, Farringdon Street, E.C.

THE BITTER CRY

OF

OUTCAST LONDON

THERE is no more hopeful sign in the Christian Church of
to-day than the increased attention which is being given by
it to the poor and outcast classes of society. Of these it has
never been wholly neglectful; if it had it would have ceased
to be Christian. But it has, as yet, only imperfectly realised
and fulfilled its mission to the poor. Until recently it has
contented itself with sustaining some outside organizations,
which have charged themselves with this special function,
or what is worse, has left the matter to individuals or to
little bands of Christians having no organization. For the
rest it has been satisfied with a superficial and inadequate
district visitation, with the more or less indiscriminate
distribution of material charities, and with opening a few
rooms here and there into which the poorer people have
been gathered, and by which a few have been rescued. All
this is good in its way and has done good; but by all only
the merest edge of the great dark region of poverty, misery,
squalor and immorality has been touched. We are not
losing sight of the London City Mission, whose agents are
everywhere, and whose noble work our investigations have
led us to value more than ever, but after all has been done
the churches are making the discovery that seething in the
very centre of our great cities, concealed by the thinnest
crust of civilization and decency, is a vast mass of moral
corruption, of heart-breaking misery and absolute godless-

ness, and that scarcely anything has been done to take into this awful slough the only influences that can purify or remove it.

Whilst we have been building our churches and solacing ourselves with our religion and dreaming that the millennium was coming, the poor have been growing poorer, the wretched more miserable, and the immoral more corrupt; the gulf has been daily widening which separates the lowest classes of the community from our churches and chapels, and from all decency and civilization. It is easy to bring an array of facts which seem to point to the opposite conclusion—to speak of the noble army of men and women who penetrate the vilest haunts, carrying with them the blessings of the gospel; of the encouraging reports published by Missions, Reformatories, Refuges, Temperance Societies; of Theatre Services, Midnight Meetings and Special Missions. But what does it all amount to? We are simply living in a fool's paradise if we suppose that all these agencies combined are doing a thousandth part of what needs to be done, a hundredth part of what *could* be done by the Church of Christ. We must face the facts; and these compel the conviction that THIS TERRIBLE FLOOD OF SIN AND MISERY IS GAINING UPON US. It is rising every day. This statement is made as the result of a long, patient and sober inquiry, undertaken for the purpose of discovering the actual state of the case and the remedial action most likely to be effective. Convinced that it is high time some combined and organized effort was made by all denominations of Christians, though not for denominational purposes, the London Congregational Union have determined to open in several of the lowest and most needy districts of the metropolis, suitable Mission Halls, as a base of operations for evangelistic work. They have accordingly made this diligent search, and some of the results are set forth in the following pages, in the hope that all who have the power may be stimulated to help the Union in the great and difficult enterprise which they have undertaken.

Two cautions it is important to bear in mind. First, the information given *does not refer to selected cases*. It simply reveals a state of things which is found in house after house, court after court, street after street. Secondly, there *has been absolutely no exaggeration*. It is a plain recital of plain facts. Indeed, no respectable printer would print, and certainly no decent family would admit even the driest statement of the horrors and infamies discovered in one brief visitation from house to house. *So far from making the worst of our facts for the purpose of appealing to emotion, we have been compelled to tone down everything, and wholly to omit what most needs to be known, or the ears and eyes of our readers would have been insufferably outraged.* Yet even this qualified narration must be to every Christian heart a loud and bitter cry, appealing for the help which it is the supreme mission of the Church to supply. It should be further stated that our investigations were made in the summer. The condition of the poor during the winter months must be very much worse.

NON-ATTENDANCE AT WORSHIP

It is perhaps scarcely necessary to say of the hundreds of thousands who compose the class referred to, that very few attend any place of worship. It is a very tame thing to say, and a very little thing compared with what must follow, but it is needful to a proper statement of our case. Before going to the lower depths, where our investigations were principally carried on, we find in the neighbourhood of Old Ford, in 147 consecutive houses, inhabited for the most part by the respectable working class, 212 families, 118 of which never, under any circumstances, attend a place of worship. Out of 2290 persons living in consecutive houses at Bow Common, only 88 adults and 47 children ever attend, and as 64 of these are connected with one Mission Hall, only 24 out of the entire number worship elsewhere. One street off Leicester Square contains 246 families, and only 12 of these are ever represented at the house of God. In another street in Pentonville, out of 100 families only 12 persons attend any sanctuary, whilst the number of attendants in one district of St. George's-in-the-East is 39 persons out of

4235. Often the numbers given of those who do attend
include such as only go once or twice a year, at some
charity distribution, so that our figures are more favourable
than the actual facts. Constantly we come across persons
who have never been to church or chapel for 20 years, 28
years, more than 30 years; and some persons as old as 64
never remember having been in a place of worship at all.
Indeed, with the exception of a very small proportion, the
idea of going has never dawned upon these people. And
who can wonder? Think of

THE CONDITION IN WHICH THEY LIVE

We do not say the condition of their homes, for how can
those places be called homes, compared with which the
lair of a wild beast would be a comfortable and healthy
spot? Few who will read these pages have any conception
of what these pestilential human rookeries are, where tens
of thousands are crowded together amidst horrors which
call to mind what we have heard of the middle passage of
the slave ship. To get into them you have to penetrate
courts reeking with poisonous and malodorous gases arising
from accumulations of sewage and refuse scattered in all
directions and often flowing beneath your feet; courts, many
of them which the sun never penetrates, which are never
visited by a breath of fresh air, and which rarely know
the virtues of a drop of cleansing water. You have to ascend
rotten staircases, which threaten to give way beneath every
step, and which, in some places, have already broken down,
leaving gaps that imperil the limbs and lives of the unwary.
You have to grope your way along dark and filthy passages
swarming with vermin. Then, if you are not driven back by
the intolerable stench, you may gain admittance to the dens
in which these thousands of beings who belong, as much as
you, to the race for whom Christ died, herd together. Have
you pitied the poor creatures who sleep under railway
arches, in carts or casks, or under any shelter which they
can find in the open air? You will see that they are to be
envied in comparison with those whose lot is to seek refuge

here. Eight feet square—that is about the average size of very many of these rooms. Walls and ceiling are black with the accretions of filth which have gathered upon them through long years of neglect. It is exuding through cracks in the boards overhead; it is running down the walls; it is everywhere. What goes by the name of a window is half of it stuffed with rags or covered by boards to keep out wind and rain; the rest is so begrimed and obscured that scarcely can light enter or anything be seen outside. Should you have ascended to the attic, where at least some approach to fresh air might be expected to enter from open or broken window, you look out upon the roofs and ledges of lower tenements, and discover that the sickly air which finds its way into the room has to pass over the putrefying carcases of dead cats or birds, or viler abominations still. The buildings are in such miserable repair as to suggest the thought that if the wind could only reach them they would soon be toppling about the heads of their occupants. As to furniture—you may perchance discover a broken chair, the tottering relics of an old bedstead, or the mere fragment of a table; but more commonly you will find rude substitutes for these things in the shape of rough boards resting upon bricks, an old hamper or box turned upside down, or more frequently still, nothing but rubbish and rags.

Every room in these rotten and reeking tenements houses a family, often two. In one cellar a sanitary inspector reports finding a father, mother, three children and four pigs! In another room a missionary found a man ill with small pox, his wife just recovering from her eighth confinement, and the children running about half naked and covered with dirt. Here are seven people living in one underground kitchen, and a little dead child lying in the same room. Elsewhere is a poor widow, her three children, and a child who had been dead thirteen days. Her husband, who was a cabman, had shortly before committed suicide. Here lives a widow and her six children, including one daughter of 29, another of 21, and a son of 27. Another apartment contains father, mother and six children, two of whom are ill with scarlet fever. In another nine brothers and sisters, from 29 years of age downwards, live, eat and sleep together. Here is a mother who turns her children into the street in the early evening because she lets her room for immoral purposes until long after midnight, when the poor little wretches creep back again if they have not found some miserable shelter elsewhere. Where there are beds they are simply heaps of dirty rags, shavings or straw, but for the most part these miserable beings huddle together upon the filthy boards. The tenant of this room is a widow, who herself occupies the only bed, and lets the floor to a married couple for 2s. 6d. per week. In many cases matters are made worse by the unhealthy occupations followed by those who dwell in these habitations. Here you are choked as you enter by the air laden with particles of the superfluous fur pulled from the skins of rabbits, rats, dogs and other animals in their preparation for the furrier. Here the smell of paste and of drying match-boxes, mingling with other sickly odours, overpowers you; or it may be the fragrance of stale fish or vegetables, not sold on the previous day, and kept in the room overnight. Even when it is possible to do so the people seldom open their windows, but if they did it is questionable whether much would be gained, for the external air is scarcely less heavily charged with poison than the atmosphere within.

Wretched as these rooms are they are beyond the means of many who wander about all day, picking up a living as they can, and then take refuge at night in one of the common lodging-houses that abound. These are often the resorts of thieves and vagabonds of the lowest types, and some are kept by receivers of stolen goods. In the kitchen men and women may be seen cooking their food, washing their clothes, or lolling about smoking and gambling. In the sleeping room are long rows of beds on each side, sometimes 60 or 80 in one room. In many cases both sexes are allowed to herd together without any attempt to preserve the commonest decency. But there is a lower depth still. Hundreds cannot even scrape together the two-pence required to secure them the privilege of herding in those sweltering common sleeping rooms, and so they huddle together upon the stairs and landings, where it is no uncommon thing to find six or eight in the early morning.

That people condemned to exist under such conditions take to drink and fall into sin is surely a matter for little surprise. We may rather say, as does one recent and reliable explorer, that they are "entitled to credit for not being twenty times more depraved than they are." One of the saddest results of this over-crowding is the inevitable association of honest people with criminals. Often is the family of an honest working man compelled to take refuge in a thieves' kitchen; in the houses where they live their rooms are frequently side by side, and continual contact with the very worst of those who have come out of our gaols is a matter of necessity. There can be no question that numbers of habitual criminals would never have become such, had they not by force of circumstances been packed together in these slums with those who were hardened in crime. Who can wonder that every evil flourishes in such hotbeds of vice and disease? Who can wonder that little children taken from these hovels to the hospital cry, when they are well, through dread of being sent back to their former misery? Who can wonder that young girls wander off into a life of immorality, which promises release from such conditions? Who can wonder that the public-house is "the Elysian field of the tired toiler?"

IMMORALITY

is but the natural outcome of conditions like these. "Marriage," it has been said, "as an institution, is not fashionable in these districts." And this is only the bare truth. Ask if the men and women living together in these rookeries are married, and your simplicity will cause a smile. Nobody knows. Nobody cares. Nobody expects that they are. In exceptional cases only could your question be answered in the affirmative. Incest is common; and no form of vice and sensuality causes surprise or attracts attention. Those who appear to be married are often separated by a mere quarrel, and they do not hesitate to form similar companionships immediately. One man was pointed out who for some years had lived with a woman, the mother of his three children. She died and in less than a week he had taken another woman in her place. A man was living with a woman in the low district called "The Mint." He went out one morning with another man for the purpose of committing a burglary and by that other man was murdered. The murderer returned saying that his companion had been caught and taken away to prison; and the same night he took the place of the murdered man. The only check upon communism in this regard is jealousy and not virtue. The vilest practices are looked upon with the most matter-of-fact indifference. The low parts of London are the sink into which the filthy and abominable from all parts of the country seem to flow. Entire courts are filled with thieves, prostitutes and liberated convicts. In one street are 35 houses, 32 of which are known to be brothels. In another district are 43 of these houses, and 428 fallen women and girls, many of them not more than 12 years of age. A neighbourhood whose population is returned at 10,100, contains 400 who follow this immoral traffic, their ages varying from 13 to 50; and of the moral degradation of the people, some idea may be formed from an incident which was brought to our notice. An East-end missionary rescued a young girl from an immoral life, and obtained for her a situation with people who were going abroad. He saw her to Southampton, and on his return was violently abused by the girl's grandmother, who had the sympathy of her neighbours, for having taken away from a poor old woman her means of subsistence.

The misery and sin caused by drink in these districts have often been told, but these horrors can never be set forth either by pen or artist's pencil. In the district of Euston Road is one public-house to every 100 people, counting men, women and children. Immediately around our chapel in Orange Street, Leicester Square, are 100 gin-palaces, most of them very large; and these districts are but samples of what exists in all the localities which we have investigated. Look into one of these glittering saloons, with its motley, miserable crowd, and you may be horrified as you think of the evil that is nightly wrought there; but contrast it with any of the abodes which you find in the fetid courts behind them, and you will wonder no longer that it is crowded. With its brightness, its excitement and its temporary forgetfulness of misery, it is a comparative heaven to tens of thousands. How can they be expected to resist its temptations? They could not live if they did not drink, even though they know that by drinking they do worse than die. All kinds of depravity have here their schools. Children who can scarcely walk are taught to steal, and mercilessly beaten if they come back from their daily expeditions without money or money's worth. Many of them are taken by the hand or carried in the arms to the gin-palace, and not seldom may you see mothers urging and compelling their tender infants to drink the fiery liquid. Lounging at the doors and lolling out of windows and prowling about street corners were pointed out several well-known members of the notorious band of "Forty Thieves," who, often in conspiracy with abandoned women, go out after dark to rob people in Oxford Street, Regent Street and other thoroughfares. Here you pass a coffee-house, there a wardrobe shop, there a tobacconist's, and there a grocer's, carrying on a legitimate trade no doubt, but a far different and more remunerative one as well, especially after evening sets in,—all traps to catch the unwary. These particulars indicate but faintly the moral influences from which the dwellers in these squalid regions have no escape, and by which is bred "infancy that knows no innocence, youth without modesty or shame, maturity that is mature in nothing but suffering and guilt, blasted old age that is a scandal on the name we bear."

Another difficulty with which we have to contend, and one in large measure the cause of what we have described, is the of these miserable outcasts. The poverty, we mean, of those who try to live honestly; for notwithstanding the sickening revelations of immorality which have been disclosed to us, those who endeavour to earn their bread by honest work far outnumber the dishonest. And it is to their infinite credit that it should be so, considering that they are daily face to face with the contrast between their wretched earnings and those which are the produce of sin. A child seven years old is known easily to make 10s. 6d. a week by thieving, but what can he earn by such work as match-box making, for which 2¼d. a gross is paid, the maker having to find his own fire for drying the boxes, and his own paste and string? Before he can gain as much as the young thief he must make 56 gross of match-boxes a week, or 1296 a day. It is needless to say that this is impossible, for even adults can rarely make more than an average of half that number. How long then must the little hands toil before they can earn the price of the scantiest meal! Women, for the work of trousers finishing (*i.e.*, sewing in linings, making button-holes and stitching on the buttons) receive 2½d. a pair, and have to find their own thread. We ask a woman who is making tweed trousers, how much she can earn in a day, and are told one shilling. But what does a day mean to this poor soul? *Seventeen hours!* From five in the morning to ten at night—no pause for meals. She eats her crust and drinks a little tea as she works, making in very truth, with her needle and thread, not her living only, but her shroud. For making men's shirts these women are paid 10d. a dozen; lawn tennis aprons, 3d. a dozen; and babies' hoods, from 1s. 6d. to 2s. 6d. a dozen. In St. George's-in-the-East large numbers of women and children, some of the latter only seven years old, are employed in sack-making, for which they get a farthing each. In one house was found a widow and her half idiot daughter making palliasses at 1¾d. each. Here is a woman who has a sick husband and a little child to look after. She is employed at shirt finishing.

at 3d. a dozen, and by the utmost effort can only earn 6d.
a day, out of which she has to find her own thread.
Another, with a crippled hand, maintains herself and a
blind husband by match-box making, for which she is
remunerated on the liberal scale mentioned above; and out
of her 2¼d. a gross she has to pay a girl a penny a gross
to help her. Others obtain at Covent Garden in the season
1d. or 2d. a peck for shelling peas, or 6d. a basket for
walnuts; and they do well if their labour brings them 10d.
or a shilling a day. With men it is comparatively speaking
no better. "My master," says one man visited by a recent
writer in the *Fortnightly Review*, "gets a pound for what
he gives me 3s. for making." And this it is easy to believe,
when we know that for a pair of fishing boots which will be
sold at three guineas, the poor workman receives 5s. 3d. if
they are made to order, or 4s. 6d. if made for stock. An
old tailor and his wife are employed in making policemen's
overcoats. They have to make, finish, hot-press, put on the
buttons, and find their own thread, and for all this they
receive 2s. 10d. for each coat. This old couple work from
half-past six in the morning until ten at night, and between
them can just manage to make a coat in two days. Here is
a mother who has taken away whatever articles of clothing
she can strip from her four little children without leaving
them absolutely naked. She has pawned them, not for
drink, but for coals and food. A shilling is all she can
procure, and with this she has bought seven pounds of coals
and a loaf of bread. We might fill page after page with
these dreary details, but they would become sadly monotonous, for it is the same everywhere. And then it should
not be forgotten how hardly upon poverty like this must
press the exorbitant demand for rent. Even the rack-renting
of Ireland, which so stirred our indignation a little while
ago, was merciful by comparison. If by any chance a
reluctant landlord can be induced to execute or pay for
some long-needed repairs, they become the occasion for
new exactions. Going through these rooms we come to one
in which a hole, as big as a man's head, has been roughly
covered, and how? A piece of board, from an old soap-

box, has been fixed over the opening by one nail, and to
the tenant has been given a yard and a half of paper with
which to cover it; and for this expenditure—perhaps 4d. at
the outside—*threepence a week has been put upon the rent.*
If this is enough to arouse our indignation, what must be
thought of the following? The two old people referred to
above have lived in one room for 14 years, during which
time it has only once been partially cleansed. The landlord
has undertaken that it shall be done shortly, and for the past
three months has been taking 6d. a week extra for rent for
what he is thus *going to do.* This is what the helpless have
to submit to; they are charged for these pestilential dens
a rent which consumes half the earnings of a family, and
leaves them no more than from 4d. to 6d. a day for food,
clothing and fire; a grinding of the faces of the poor which
could scarcely be paralleled in lands of slavery and of
notorious oppression. This, however, is not all; for even
these depths of poverty and degradation are reached by
the Education Act, and however beneficent its purpose, it
bears with cruel weight upon the class we have described,
to whom twopence or a penny a week for the school fees
of each of three or four children, means so much lack of
bread.

Amidst such poverty and squalor it is inevitable that one
should be constantly confronted with scenes of

HEART-BREAKING MISERY—

misery so pitiful that men whose daily duty it has been for
years to go in and out amongst these outcasts, and to be
intimately acquainted with their sufferings, and who might,
therefore, be supposed to regard with comparatively little
feeling that which would overwhelm an unaccustomed
spectator, sometimes come away from their visits so
oppressed in spirit and absorbed in painful thought, that
they know not whither they are going. How these devoted
labourers can pursue their work at all is a marvel, especially
when it is remembered that the misery they actually see
suggests to them the certain existence of so much more

which no human eye discovers. Who can even imagine the suffering which lies behind a case like the following? A poor woman in an advanced stage of consumption, reduced almost to a skeleton, lives in a single room with a drunken husband and five children. When visited she was eating a few green peas. The children were gone to gather some sticks wherewith a fire might be made to boil four potatoes which were lying on the table, and which would constitute the family dinner for the day. Or, take another case, related by Rev. Archibald Brown, who, with his missionaries is doing a noble work amongst the poor in the east of London. People had doubted the accuracy of reports presented by the missionaries, and he accordingly devoted a considerable time to personal visitation and inquiry. He found case after case proving that but little of the wretchedness had been told, and here is a *fair specimen.* At the top of an otherwise empty house lived a family; the husband had gone to try and find some work. The mother, 29 years of age, was sitting on the only chair in the place in front of a grate, destitute of any fire. She was nursing a baby only six weeks old, that had never had anything but one old rag round it. The mother had nothing but a gown on, and that dropping to pieces; it was all she had night or day. There were six children under 13 years of age. They were barefooted, and the few rags on them scarcely covered their nakedness. In this room, where was an unclothed infant, the ceiling was in holes. An old bedstead was in the place, and seven sleep in it at night, the eldest girl being on the floor.

This is bad, but it is not the worst. In a room in Wych Street, on the third floor, over a marine store dealer's, there was, a short time ago, an inquest as to the death of a little baby. A man, his wife and three children were living in that room. The infant was the second child who had died, poisoned by the foul atmosphere; and this dead baby was cut open in the one room where its parents and brothers and sisters lived, ate and slept, *because the parish had no mortuary and no room in which post mortems could be performed!* No wonder that the jurymen who went to view the body sickened at the frightful exhalations. This case was given by Mr. G. R. Sims, in his papers on "How the Poor Live;" but all the particulars are found in the dry newspaper reports of the inquest. In another miserable room are eight destitute children. Their father died a short time ago, and "on going into the house to-day," says the missionary, "the mother was lying in her coffin." Here is a filthy attic, containing only a broken chair, a battered saucepan and a few rags. On a dirty sack in the centre of the room sits a neglected, ragged, bare-legged little baby girl of four. Her father is a militiaman, and is away. Her mother is out all day and comes home late at night more or less drunk, and this child is left in charge of the infant that we see crawling about the floor; left for six or eight hours at a stretch—hungry, thirsty, tired, but never daring to move from her post. And this is the kind of sight which may be seen in a Christian land where it is criminal to ill-treat a horse or an ass.

The child-misery that one beholds is the most heart-rending and appalling element in these discoveries; and of this not the least is the misery inherited from the vice of drunken and dissolute parents, and manifest in the stunted, misshapen, and often loathsome objects that we constantly meet in these localities. From the beginning of their life they are utterly neglected; their bodies and rags are alive with vermin; they are subjected to the most cruel treatment; many of them have never seen a green field, and do not know what it is to go beyond the streets imme-diately around them, and they often pass the whole day without a morsel of food. Here is one of three years old picking up some dirty pieces of bread and eating them. We go in at the doorway where it is standing and find a little girl twelve years old. "Where is your mother?" "In the madhouse." "How long has she been there?" "Fifteen months." "Who looks after you?" The child, who is sitting at an old table making match-boxes, replies, "I look after my little brothers and sisters as well as I can." "Where is your father? Is he in work?" "He has been out of work three weeks, but he has gone to a job of two days this morning." Another house visited contains nine motherless children. The mother's death was caused by witnessing one of her children being run over. The eldest is only fourteen years old. All live in one small room, and there is one bed for five. Here is a poor woman deserted by her husband and left with three little children. One met with an accident a few days ago and broke his arm. He is lying on a shake-down in one corner of the room, with an old sack round him. And here, in a cellar kitchen, are nine little ones. You can scarcely see across the room for smoke and dirt. They are without food and have scarcely any clothing.

It is heart-crushing to think of the misery suggested by such revelations as these; and there is something unspeakably pathetic in the brave patience with which the poor not seldom endure their sufferings, and the tender sympathy which they show toward each other. Where, amongst the well-conditioned, can anything braver and kinder be found than this? A mother, whose children are the cleanest and tidiest in the Board School which they attend, was visited. It was found that, though she had children of her own, she had taken in a little girl, whose father had gone off tramping in search of work. She was propped up in a chair, looking terribly ill, but in front of her, in another chair, was the wash-tub, and the poor woman was making a feeble effort to wash and wring out some of the children's things. She was dying from dropsy, scarcely able to breathe and enduring untold agony, but to the very last striving to keep her little ones clean and tidy. A more touching sight it would be difficulty to present; we might, however, unveil many more painful ones, but must content ourselves with saying that the evidence we have gathered from personal observation more than justifies the words of the writer before referred to, that "there are (*i.e.*, in addition to those who find their way to our hospitals) men and women who lie and die day by day in their wretched single rooms, sharing all the family trouble, enduring the hunger and the cold, and waiting without hope, without a single ray of comfort, until God curtains their staring eyes with the merciful film of death."

WHAT IT IS PROPOSED TO DO

That something needs to be done for this pitiable outcast population must be evident to all who have read these particulars as to their condition—at least, to all who believe them. We are quite prepared for incredulity. Even what we have indicated seems all too terrible to be true. But we have sketched only in faintest outline. Far more vivid must be our colours, deeper and darker far the shades, if we are to present a truthful picture of "Outcast London;" and so far as we have been able to go we are prepared with evidence, not only to prove every statement, but to show that these statements represent the general condition of thousands upon thousands in this metropolis. Incredulity is not the only difficulty in the way of stirring up Christian people to help. Despair of success in any such undertaking may paralyse many. We shall be pointed to the fact that without State interference nothing effectual can be accomplished upon any large scale. And *it is* a fact. These wretched people must live somewhere. They must live near the centres where their work lies. They cannot afford to go out by train or tram into the suburbs; and how, with their poor emaciated, starved bodies, can they be expected—in addition to working twelve hours or more, for a shilling, or less—to walk three or four miles each way to take and fetch? It is notorious that the Artizans Dwellings Act has, in some respects, made matters worse for them. Large spaces have been cleared of fever-breeding rookeries, to make way for the building of decent habitations, but the rents of these are far beyond the means of the abject poor. They are driven to crowd more closely together in the few stifling places still left to them; and so Dives makes a richer harvest out of their misery, buying up property condemned as unfit for habitation, and turning it into a gold-mine because the poor must have shelter somewhere, even though it be the shelter of a living tomb.

The State must make short work of this iniquitous traffic, and secure for the poorest the rights of citizenship;

the right to live in something better than fever dens; the right to live as something better than the uncleanest of brute beasts. This must be done before the Christian missionary can have much chance with them. But because we cannot do all we wish, are we to do nothing? Even as things are something can be accomplished. Is no lifeboat to put out and no life-belt to be thrown because only half a dozen out of the perishing hundreds can be saved from the wreck? The very records which supply the sad story we have been telling, give also proofs of what can be done by the Gospel and by Christian love and tact and devotion. Gladly do many of these poor creatures receive the Gospel. Little match-box makers are heard singing at their toil, "One more day's work for Jesus." "If only mother was a Christian we should all be happy," said one; and on his miserable bed, amidst squalor and want and pain, a poor blind man dies with the prayer upon his lips, "Jesus, lover of my soul, Let me to Thy bosom fly." Another writes, "You have filled my heart with joy, and my little room with sunshine." A second, who now regularly attends a place of worship, says, speaking of the visits of the missionary, "Before he came to visit me I used to sit and make match-boxes on Sunday, but a word now and then has enabled me to look up to the Lord. I don't feel like the same person." Another who himself became a mission- ary to his own class, and exercised great power over them whenever he spoke, was able to say, "I was as bad as any of you, but the Lord Jesus had mercy upon me, and has made me better and so happy." This man had been a "coal- whipper" of notoriously evil life, and was rescued through his casually going into a room in one of the courts of which we have spoken, where a missionary was holding a meeting. Such results should rebuke our faithlessness. Even in these dark and noisome places the lamp of Life may be kindled; even from these miry spots bright gems may be snatched, worth all the labour and all the cost.

It is little creditable to us that all our wealth and effort should be devoted to providing for the spiritual needs of those who are comfortably conditioned, and none of it

expended upon the abject poor. It is true that we have not
half done our duty to any class, but this fact is no justification of our having wholly neglected this rescue work. To
shut up our compassion against those who need it most,
because we have not yet done our duty to those who need
it less, is a course that we should find it hard to justify
to our Master and Lord. His tones were ever those of pity-
ing love even to the most sinful outcast, but would they
not gather sternness as He met us with the rebuke: "This
ought ye to have done, and not to have left the other
undone"? An "exceeding bitter cry" is this which goes up
to heaven from the misery of London against the apathy
of the Church. It is time that Christians opened their ears
to it and let it sink down into their hearts. Many pressing
needs are taxing the resources of the London Congregational Union, but the Committee feel that this work
amongst the poor must no longer be neglected, and that they
must do all they can to arouse the Churches of their order
to undertake their share of responsibility. They have determined to take immediate action. Having selected three of
the very worst districts in London, from which many of the
foregoing facts have been gathered, they have resolved at
once to begin operations in the very heart of them. No
denominational purpose will sway them, except that they
will try to awaken their own denomination to a sense of its
duty; but there will be no attempt to make Congrega-
tionalists or to present Congregationalism. Deeper, broader
and simpler must this work be than any which can be
carried on upon denominational lines. In such a forlorn
hope there is no room for sectarianism. The Gospel of the
love of Christ must be presented in its simplest form, and
the one aim in everything must be to rescue and not to
proselytize. Help will be thankfully welcomed from whatever quarter it may come, and help will be freely given to
other workers in the same field, if only by any means some
may be saved. It is impossible here and yet to give details
as to the methods which it is proposed to pursue; suffice
it to say that in each district a Mission Hall will be erected,
or some existing building transformed into a Hall having

appliances and conveniences requisite for the successful prosecution of the Mission. Services and meetings of all kinds will be arranged, and, as far as possible, an agency for house to house visitation organized. An attempt must be made to relieve in some wise and practical, though very limited way, the abounding misery, whilst care is taken to prevent the abuse of charity. In this matter the injudicious and inexperienced may easily do more harm than good, pauperising the people whom they wish to help, and making hypocrites instead of Christians. To indicate what we mean we may mention one case pointed out to us of a woman who attended three different places of worship on the Sunday and some others during the week, because she obtained charitable help from all. But we cannot on this account refuse to try some means of mitigating the suffering with which we come into contact. Therefore this must be attempted along with whatever other means the Committee, in conference with those who have had long experience of this work, may think likely to answer the end they have before them. Their hope is that at least some, even of the lowest and worst, may be gathered in; and their aim will be to make as many of these as they can missionaries to the others; for manifestly those who have been accustomed to speak to and work amongst a somewhat better section of the community will not be so likely to labour sucessfully amongst these outcasts as will those who have themselves been of their number. The three districts already fixed upon are, as it will be understood, intended only to afford a field for the immediate commencement of this beneficent work. Other districts will be occupied as funds come in and the resources of the Committee are enlarged; but even the comparatively limited operations already undertaken will necessitate so great an expenditure and require so much aid from those who are qualified for the work, that they cannot wisely attempt more at present. For not only will the cost and furnishing of Halls and of carrying on the work be very large, but a relief fund will be needed as indicated above. The Committee, therefore, can only hope to carry forward with any success the project to which they have already put their hands, by the really devoted help of the churches which they represent.

DESCRIPTION OF THE DISTRICTS

The district known as Collier's Rents is one of the three to which attention will first be given, and the old chapel, long disused, is now in the builders' hands and will soon be ready for opening, not as a chapel, but as a bright, comfortable, and in every way suitable Hall. It would be impossible to find a building better situated for working among the very poor and degraded than this. It stands in a short street, leading out of Long Lane, Bermondsey, the locality in which were recently found the bodies of nine infants, which had been deposited in a large box at the foot of some stairs in an undertaker's shop. There are around the Hall some 650 families, or 3250 people, living in 123 houses. The houses are largely occupied by costermongers, birdcatchers, street singers, liberated convicts, thieves and prostitutes. There are many low lodging-houses in the neighbourhood of the worst type. Some of them are tenanted chiefly by thieves, and one was pointed out which is kept by a receiver of stolen goods. In some cases two of the houses are united by means of a passage which affords a ready method of escape in case of police interference.

Turning out of one of these streets you enter a narrow passage, about ten yards long and three feet wide. This leads into a court eighteen yards long and nine yards wide. Here are twelve houses of three rooms each, and containing altogether 36 families. The sanitary condition of the place is indescribable. A large dust-bin charged with all manner of filth and putrid matter stands at one end of the court, and four water-closets at the other. In this confined area all the washing of these 36 families is done, and the smell of the place is intolerable. Entering a doorway you go up six or seven steps into a long passage, so dark that you have to grope your way by the clammy, dirt-encrusted wall, and then you find a wooden stair, some of the steps of which are broken through. Ascending as best you can, you gain admission to one of the rooms. You find that although the front and back of the house are of brick, the rooms are separated only by partitions of boards, some of which are an inch apart. There are no locks on the doors and it would seem that they can only be fastened on the outside by padlock. In this room to which we have come an old bed, on which are some evil-smelling rags, is, with the exception of a broken chair, the only article of furniture. Its sole occupant just now is a repulsive, half-drunken Irishwoman. She is looking at some old ragged garments in hope of being able to raise something upon them at the pawnshop, and being asked if she is doing this because she is poor, she gets into a rage and cries, "Call me poor? I have got half a loaf of bread in the house, and a little milk;" and then from a heap of rubbish in one corner, she pulls out a putrid turkey, utterly unfit for human food, which she tells us she is going to cook for dinner. This woman has just "done seven days" for an assault upon a police officer. We find that she has a husband, but he spends almost all his money at the public-house. Rooms such as this are let furnished (!) at 3s. 6d. and 4s. a week, or 8d. a night, and we are told that the owner is getting from 50 to 60 per cent. upon his money.

And this is a specimen of the neighbourhood. Reeking courts, crowded public-houses, low lodging-houses and numerous brothels are to be found all around. Even the cellars are tenanted. Poverty, rags and dirt everywhere. The air is laden with disease-breeding gases. The missionaries who labour here, are constantly being attacked by some malady or other resulting from blood poisoning, and their tact and courage are subjected to the severest tests. In going about these alleys and courts no stranger is safe if alone. Not long ago a doctor on his rounds was waylaid by a number of women, who would not let him pass to see his patient until he had given them money; and a bible-woman, visiting "Kent Street," was robbed of most of her clothing. Even the police seldom venture into some parts of the district except in company. Yet bad as it is there are elements of hopefulness which encourage us to believe that our work will not be in vain. Many of its denizens would gladly break away from the dismal, degrading life they are leading, if only a way were made for them to do so; as it is they are hemmed in and chained down by their surroundings in hopeless and helpless misery.

Such is Collier's Rents. To describe the other two localities where our work is to be commenced, in Ratcliff and Shadwell, would, in the main, be but to repeat the same heart-sickening story. Heart-sickening but soul-stirring. We have opened but a little way the door that leads into this plague-house of sin and misery and corruption, where men and women and little children starve and suffer and perish, body and soul. But even the glance we have got is a sight to make one weep. We shall not wonder if some, shuddering at the revolting spectacle, try to persuade themselves that such things cannot be in Christian England, and that what they have looked upon is some dark vision conjured by a morbid pity and a desponding faith. To such we can only say, Will you venture to come with us and see for yourselves the ghastly reality? Others, looking on, will believe, and pity, and despair. But another vision will be seen by many, and in this lies our hope—a vision of Him who had "compassion upon the multitude because they were as sheep having no shepherd," looking, with Divine pity in His eyes, over this outcast London, and then turning to the consecrated host of His Church with the appeal, "Whom shall we send and who will go for us?"

October, 1883.

Oh, Thou, who once on earth, beneath the weight
Of our mortality, didst live and move,
The incarnation of profoundest love;
Who on the Cross that love didst consummate—
Whose deep and ample fulness could embrace
The poorest, meanest, of our fallen race:
How shall we e'er that boundless debt repay?
By long loud prayers in gorgeous temples said?
By rich oblations on Thine altars laid?
Ah, no! not thus Thou didst appoint the way.
When Thou wast bowed our human woe beneath,
Then, as a legacy, Thou didst bequeath
Earth's sorrowing children to our ministry—
And, as we do to them we do to Thee.

ANNE CHARLOTTE LYNCH.